COMICS
An Illustrated History

For Justin and Ben...

COMICS
An Illustrated History

Alan and Laurel Clark

A Green Wood Book

Text copyright
© 1991 Alan and Laurel Clark

Copyright © 1991 The Green Wood
Publishing Company Ltd

ISBN
1 872532 55 1

Design and typesetting
Playne Books

Printed and bound in Hong Kong

The Green Wood Publishing
Company Ltd
6/7 Warren Mews
London
W1P 5DJ

Contents

The history of the comic

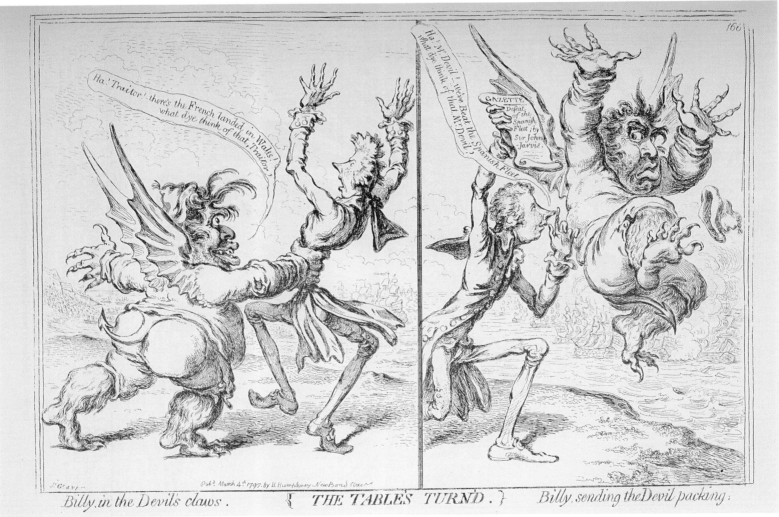

Early comic strip format, complete with word balloons, in a twin-panelled cartoon by British caricaturist James Gillray: 1797

Comics as we know them today have been a familar feature for a long time. And comic art has always been with us. Historians would cite cave drawings, Egyptian hieroglyphics and the Bayeux tapestry as early examples of the medium. But the comic itself has more recent origins. Moreover, it has not been one country alone that has played a part in the comic's development, although some nations have succeeded in popularizing it more than others. It has been truly an international effort.

In the eighteenth century the celebrated English artists William Hogarth, James Gillray and Thomas Rowlandson used comic art to comment on politics, fashion and the social scene. The single drawings that these artists produced (often incorporating word-balloons) were published in the form of prints, some in black and white and others hand-coloured. The prints were then sold in shops all over London. The work of these artists, and that of their contemporaries, also became popular on the Continent.

Sometimes prints were gathered together and published in magazine format. Viewed sequentially, these could be regarded as an early form of comic. The principal feature of these often scurrilous cartoons was caricature, a practice that is reported to have started in Italy.

Caricature was also a mainstay of the English magazine **Punch**, dating from 1841. Inspired by a similar French publication, the business of **Punch** was humour, much of it consisting of pictures and far

6

Aber schon mit viel Vergnügen
Sehen sie die Brezeln liegen.

Schwapp! da liegen sie im Brei.

Knacks! da bricht der Stuhl entzwei;

38

Ganz von Kuchenteig umhüllt,
Stehn sie da als Jammerbild. –

39

An excerpt from the adventures of
Wilhelm Busch's young demons,
Max und Moritz, ending, typically,
in comical disaster

too good to be wasted on only one printing: the magazine's drawings and cartoons were frequently published in book form.

One of **Punch**'s many imitators was **Judy** (1867) which introduced the character *Ally Sloper,* who became a huge star, eventually having his own weekly title: the world's first regularly appearing comic character to do so.

On the Continent comics began as 'picture sheets'. These were single tabloid-size pages with stories that were told in pictures on one side. Usually these picture sheets were numbered — handy if it was a serial; vital if you were a nineteenth-century collector (and human nature rules that there would have been some!)

Picture sheets were especially popular in France and Germany. In Germany, in the 1860s, two of the most popular picture sheet characters were **Max und Moritz**, created by artist Wilhelm Busch.

By the latter half of the nineteenth century, picture sheets were being exported to the United States, no doubt following the French and German emigrants who used to read them in their home countries. But long before that, in the 1840s, the firm of D.C. Johnston of Boston had issued a publication entitled **Scraps** which was a recognizable evolutionary 'staging post' on the way to being a comic. Later, in 1871, the adventures of Wilhelm Busch's **Max und Moritz** were translated and published.

More lethal mayhem from bad boys Max und Moritz

Victorian superstar Ally Sloper carries in the Christmas turkey. Note that the comic also serves as a Life Assurance policy, a popular sales ploy of the era

These two demonic German bad boys would have been familiar to the many German immigrants who had made their home in the USA. Indeed, these had reached a sizeable enough population for a man named Joseph Keppler to start a German-language weekly called **Puck** in 1876. This venture proved successful enough for him to launch in the following year an English language version.

By the 1880s **Puck** had been joined by rival publications **Judge** (1880) and **Life** (1883). Besides reprinting comic strips and cartoons in approximations of the comic form, these three famous American magazines were responsible for introducing within their pages some of the world's greatest practitioners of comic art; among them were Rudolph Dirks, Richard Outcault and Frederick Opper.

In the mid-1890s Joseph Pulitzer (of Pulitzer-prize fame), publisher of the **New York World**, provided the money and the push towards the development of cheap colour lithography. The **World** featured a single-panel cartoon which was called *Hogan's Alley* and starred *The Yellow Kid*, America's first comic character to appear as a regular feature.

Pulitzer's great rival, William Randolph Hearst, launched in 1897 a colour supplement to his **New York Journal** called the **American Humorist**. One of the star attractions was *The Katzenjammer Kids*, based on Hearst's favourite child-

PUCK.

YANKEE NOTIONS EUROPE!

EUROPEAN NOTIONS OF AMERICAN MANNERS AND CUSTOMS.

*A centre page spread from the US **Puck**, dated 16 November 1881, drawn by Frederick Opper. Here Opper pokes fun at Europe's notions of American manners and customs: a comic view of internationalism with (bottom right) a revealing dig at **Puck**'s transatlantic cousin, **Punch***

hood reading: Wilhelm Busch's **Max und Moritz**. Hugely successful, it is still running, making it the oldest comic strip in existence. Reprinted in book form many times and syndicated in dozens of countries, it remains a perfect example of how comics can influence one another on an international level.

On the British side of the Atlantic, it was the enterprising publisher James Henderson who produced the first true British comic, **Funny Folks**, in 1874. It was superbly printed in black and white on eight

tabloid pages. Nearly a decade later, in 1893, Henderson issued his second comic weekly, **Scraps**, perhaps an accidental borrowing of D.C. Johnston's US title of more than forty years before. However, there was nothing accidental about the plagiarism of the content, which was borrowed wholesale from **Puck**, **Judge** and **Life**.

Enterprising though Henderson was, his achievements could never be compared to those of his ex-writer, Alfred Harmsworth (later better known as Lord Northcliffe).

Harmsworth started his publishing business in 1888, launching his first comic title two years later: **Comic Cuts**, dated 17 May 1890. He followed it up with scores of comic titles, many of which — **Comic Cuts** included — lasted for decades. Henderson and Harmsworth set the style for the British comic as it was to remain for the next century.

The British news-stand comic was similar in format to the American newspaper comic supplement. US newspapers began Sunday publication in the 1880s; comic supple-

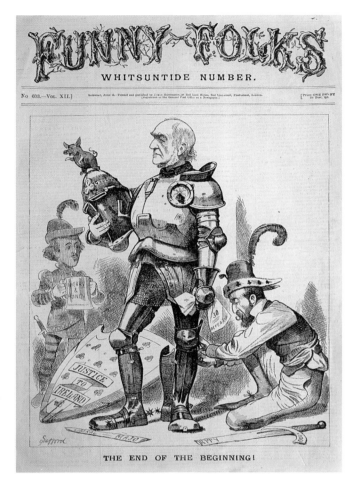

Two famous Victorian weeklies, both published by James Henderson of London: **Funny Folks** *featured splendid political cartoons on its front page drawn by John Stafford;* **Scraps** *contents included a number of US reprints*

ments were introduced during the 1890s and were common to most newspapers by the turn of the century. The tradition has lasted to this day. But any attempts to sell supplement-style comics on the American news-stands — and there have been a few — have always met with failure.

Reprints of US comics in book form appeared fairly regularly, although it took publishers some time to decide on a set format. In 1899 E.P. Dutton & Co. of New York issued **Funny Folks**, a hard-cover volume (measuring 12 x 16 inches) featuring comic material previously published in **Puck**. The next ten years saw a proliferation of similar books issued by several publishers, with many of them reprinting comic strips from the Sunday newspaper supplements at the rate of six panels per page, exactly half of a Sunday comic strip.

One of the publishers, Cupples and Leon, experimented with a different format. They limited the number of pictures to four per page, making the books square and therefore easier to handle. Again, the reprints were taken from Sunday newspaper supplements, although without the colour. These black-and-white comic books were still being issued by Cupples and Leon and their competitors well into the 1930s.

It was not until 1933, however, that the American comic book arrived in its definitive form. Max Gaines, a salesman with the Eastern Color Printing Company, was the first to have the bright idea of reprinting strips from newspaper supplements in the format we know today.

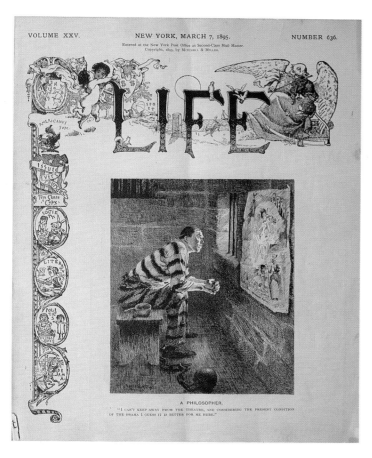

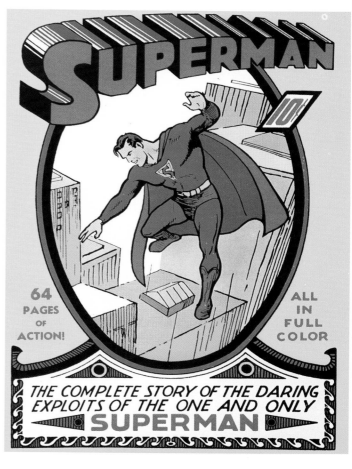

Life *in 1895 was one of the three premier cartoon publications in the USA. Inside was featured work by some of the best penmen of the era*

Following his appearance in **Action Comics** *in 1938, Superman was given his own title the following year. It was the beginning of a boom*

He instructed his printer to fold into quarters standard-size newspaper sheets, and then to separate, trim, append a cover and staple these.

At a stroke, Gaines created the format of the American comic book which has stood now for nearly sixty years. He called his venture **Funnies on Parade**; and the thirty-two pages of reprints were printed in full colour; only the cover art was original. Gaines marketed his comic via Proctor and Gamble: all 10,000 copies were given away free with purchases of the company's products.

The following year the Eastern Color Printing Company issued **Famous Funnies** (July 1934), the first American comic book to be sold on a newsstand. Its sixty-four pages in full colour sold for ten cents. These too were all reprints. But it was left to Major Malcolm Wheeler-Nicholson — a not very businesslike businessman — to make the imaginative leap forward and begin publishing non-reprint material.

His company, National Allied Publications (later 'DC'), issued **New Fun No. 1**, its cover date February 1935.

National Allied Publications became a highly successful publisher, particularly when it initiated a line of superhero comic books, starting with **Action Comics** in June 1938. The first issue introduced *Superman*, now famous all over the world and one of the most recognizable comic characters. The following year the adventures of *Batman* began to appear in **Detective Comics**, a monthly begun by National in 1937.

From this point on, the shape of the American comic book was firmly established.

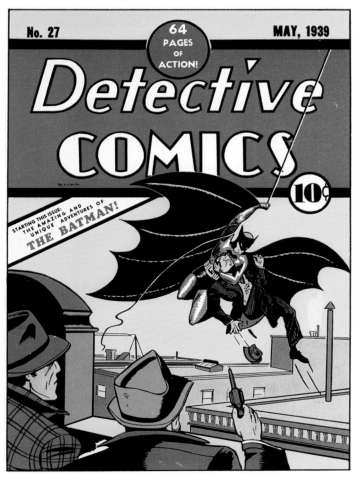

The Batman *swung into action in* **Detective Comics** *No. 27, issued in May 1939*

A year later, in 1940, the costumed sleuth had been joined by a boy companion, Robin, and had been given his own title

So, indeed, was the superhero. Both the format and the genre were to gain worldwide popularity.

Countries outside the US had not stood by idly. In 1905 the comic magazine **O Tico Tico** was published for the first time in Brazil and **Tokyo Puck** was founded in Japan; then in 1908 the comic weekly **L'Epatant** began in Paris. Newspaper strips had been started in Australia, Mexico, Italy, Finland, Sweden and many more countries. All of them inspired reprint collections from time to time.

Some European newspapers began to include supplements. One such was the Belgian **Le Petit Vingtième** (supplement to the daily **Le Vingtième**) which in 1929 introduced the character *Tintin*, the creation of Georges Rémi (Hergé). Tintin's adventures first appeared in comic book form the following year. Other huge successes on the European scene have been Marten Toonder's *Tom Poes (Tom Puss)*, a character created in 1938, and *Asterix*, René Goscinny and Albert Uderzo's creation for the French comic weekly **Pilote** in 1959.

Until the Second World War the world saw much of British comics, circulating freely throughout 'an Empire on which the sun never set'. British colonies and dominions around the globe were sent regular supplies of the latest weeklies from Farringdon Street, where stood the offices of Britain's biggest publisher, the Amalgamated Press. But a wartime shortage of ink and paper led to the cancellation of many titles, and UK exports came to a halt.

As the British supplies stopped, US shipments started. US comic books

It is easy to see why readers thrilled to Superman's early adventures with the exciting sequence shown above. Written by Jerry Siegel and drawn by Joe Shuster, the dynamic man of steel beats a locomotive to carry out an amazing rescue

— not affected by the ink drought and paper famine — were produced in hundreds of thousands. Many were exported; others found their way abroad via US servicemen and then to local outlets. Unsold US issues, together with remaindered pulp magazines, were used as ballast in empty ships crossing the Atlantic. These eventually found their way to the public through cheap chain stores and street markets. Thus the American comic books became extremely popular worldwide. A combination of their attractive format and full colour

stories that could be enjoyed by a wide age range would continue to ensure their lasting success.

In more recent times European-produced graphic novels have been much admired by the USA, and the Americans have now adapted this style of publication for the more serious aficionados.

Comics have moved on from the days when they were produced simply to amuse children and sell newspapers (although they still do both). They are now an integral part

of our society, used for everything from advertising to education, from entertainment to social comment.

Although every country has its own fine comic artists, the Americans undoubtedly produce the most renowned comics; and it is they, above all, who have popularized them. The United States is said to have given the world three popular art forms this century: movies, jazz and comics. Few would complain that this was unfair comment. And like jazz and the movies, comics would seem to be here to stay.

GRAND FREE GIFT FOR YOU WITH THIS COPY!

The Kinema Comic 2d

Every Wednesday

No. 458.　　Vol. 9.　　February 2nd, 1929.

PAPER FOR BOYS! SPACE GUN NOVELTY—

TIGER

The SPORT and ADVENTURE PICTURE STORY WEEKLY

ROY POUNCED ON A LOOSE PASS—
IT'S ALL YOURS, ROY!
ROY'S TWINKLING FE AS HE WAS TACKLED

Nº1—FEB. 7th, 1953.

THE TOPPER

PRICE 3D

SCREAMINGLY
:: FUNNY ::

COMIC DISGUISE
ABSOLUTELY FREE.

No. 1—JAN. 21st. 1956.

The BEEZER, January 21, 1956

THE BEEZER

3D EVERY TUESDAY

Film Fun

our Grand Free Gift

No. 254.　Vol. 5.

GINGER

BRR! IT'S C-C-COLD!

I NEED HEAT
ALL ROUND!

I'M FROZEN, BUT
THAT HORSE
LOOKS HOT!

AN I WARM MY COLD
ANDS ON YOUR
HOT HORSE?

SUPER NEW PAPER! FREE SPORTS STARS ALBUM INSIDE!

BIG COMPETITION
1,000 PRIZES

LION

KING OF
PICTURE
STORY
PAPERS

3D

No. 1.

WEEK ENDING FEBRUARY 23, 1952

OUTLAW

EACH DAY THE PRISONERS WERE MARCHED THROUGH THE WEIRD TITAN JUNGLE
FROM THEIR CAMP TO THE MINES. THEY WERE CLOSELY GUARDED BY
GEEKS ARMED WITH ATOMIC PARALYSERS

BRITISH COMICS

The first British Comic Art was caricature and its most famous early exponent William Hogarth (1697-1764). He was first and foremost a painter of considerable ability but turned to the production of moralistic prints to supplement his income. These were single drawings, usually with a caption below. Caricature in itself was nothing new; it had long been imported from Europe. But Hogarth managed to produce something different: an English school, rather than a poor imitation of the European style.

As with many of the best cartoonists, Hogarth believed in depicting extremes. Activities he frowned upon (such as the drinking of gin) were pictured as the depths of depravity; practices of which he approved (like the supping of beer) were revealed as the pinnacles of happiness. His most celebrated works were the series of prints *The Rake's Progress*, *The Harlot's Progress* and *Marriage à la Mode*. In effect these were sermons of the

hell-and-damnation variety. As each of these presented a series of sequential pictures that told a story, they might also be regarded as early comic strips.

Two famous successors were James Gillray (1757-1815) and Thomas Rowlandson (1756-1827). Gillray changed the nature of the print and broadened its appeal. Where Hogarth was moralistic, Gillray turned his attention to the political and social scene, attacking the establishment with wit and bite. No one

In 1735 William Hogarth's **A Rake's Progress** *told the story of the Rake's life of excesses*

was spared his pen: the royal family, politicians, prominent socialites and institutions. As a result he made some enemies. Mrs Humphrey's Print Shop (above which he lived) was the main retailer of his works and had its window smashed by at least one angry subject. Perhaps what saved him from total loathing by those he caricatured was the war against Napoleon. He used his skill to lampoon the French and is credited as having played a vital part in the war effort.

Rowlandson was technically a better artist but his work lacked the bite of Gillray. His pictures were gentler, his satire and caricatures not nearly so vicious. But the scenes he depicted — taverns, landscapes, meeting places, and so on — were drawn with commendable accuracy. He also created the first regularly appearing character in picture form in **The Tours of Doctor Syntax** (1798). The Doctor's tours were published in book form in 1812, 1820 and 1822.

Gillray's life came to an unhappy end: he went slightly mad, made an unsuccessful attempt at suicide and died shortly afterwards. During this period his work suffered and he was unable to finish some of his prints. He was assisted in completing them by two young brothers, George and Robert Cruikshank. After Gillray's death, each built up an independent reputation. Of the two, George (1792-1878) was the better artist and enjoyed a longer career. He began as a caricaturist — taking over from Gillray in many respects — but he eventually found it more profitable, and more socially acceptable, to enter the more genteel provinces of art by turning to book and periodical illustration.

Caricatures were likewise a feature of picture sheets (also known as broadsheets). These consisted of one tabloid page with several pictures printed on one side and were available in plain or coloured versions.

Originally imported from Europe, in time they were issued by British publishers as well; early titles included **The Glasgow Looking Glass** (1825), **McLean's Monthly Sheet of Caricatures** (1830) and **Every Body's Album** (1834). Sometimes collected together in bound editions, and occasionally featuring sequential pictures, broadsheets were clearly ancestors of the comic.

A cynical view of Parliamentary candidates, complete with word balloons, from the first issue of **Punch***, 18 July 1841*

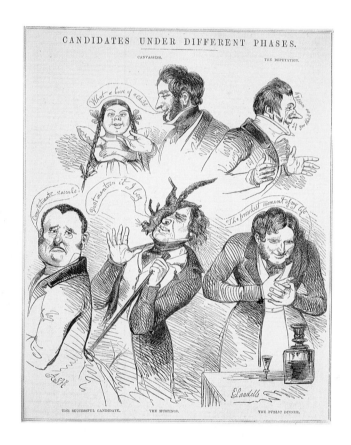

From caricature to comic strip

On 18 July 1841 the magazine **Punch** was launched in London. It echoed the success of the French satirical weekly, **Le Charivari**, and paid the latter due tribute by subtitling itself **The London Charivari**. The most famous of its early contributors was John Leech. Together with the editor, Mark Lemon, he had the distinction of being the first to apply the word 'cartoon' to what had previously been known as caricatures.

Indeed, Leech and **Punch** were mainly responsible for the trend away from caricature and toward straightforward likeness. **Punch** also tidied up the symbolism of the caricaturists (such as the British Lion and John Bull), making it more respectable and employing a more dramatic form of comic illustration. From its earliest days, **Punch** featured sets of related drawings which approached the concept of the comic strip. Leech himself drew a series of adventures of *Mr Briggs* – a comic strip in all but name.

Naturally, **Punch** spawned many imitators, the better-known of which were **Fun** (1861) and **Judy** (1867). The former had some excellent cartoons-cum-comic-strips: foremost of its illustrators was J.F. Sullivan (1853-1936) who created a long-running series called *The British Working Man*, told in sequential pictures with captions. These, and some of his other works, were later collected together and published in booklet form.

On 14 August 1867, **Judy** (subtitled **The London Serio Comic Journal**) introduced *Ally Sloper* to the public. Ally Sloper was a Micawber-like bottle-nosed rogue whose trademarks were a top hat and an umbrella. His name was taken from Victorian slang – from a term used to describe someone in financial straits who 'sloped off' down alleys whenever the rent collector was on his rounds.

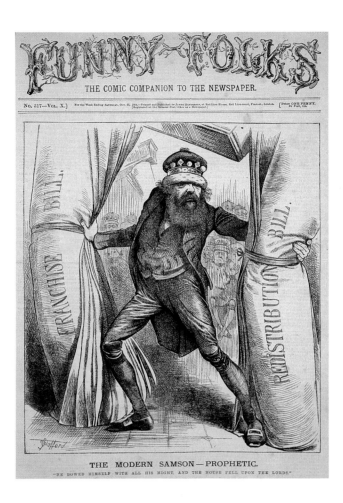

Funny Folks, James Henderson's popular 'comic companion to the Newspaper', ran from 12 December 1874 until 28 April 1894. The magnificent front-page cartoon is by John Stafford

Methods of reproduction were important in the evolution of comic art and the comic strip itself. Gillray and Rowlandson had to display their ribaldry by means of copperplate engraving: once a picture was drawn it had to be redrawn (with an etching needle) on the surface of the plate, which was coated with a thin layer of acid-resistant substance. This exposed the copper and the plate would be immersed in acid so that the exposed areas were eaten away. Ink was applied and held by the grooves in the plate. The paper was then pressed firmly on to the plate and a print completed. It was a painstaking process, often carried out by the artist himself.

It is interesting, if a little sad, to note that many of the printmakers' plates survived until the First World War. Then they were seized upon as a valuable source of copper and

melted down to make bomb fuses. Probably Gillray and his like would have approved!

Wood engraving was similarly restrictive, although it was rarely carried out by the artists themselves. Although the medium did not lend itself to finesse, with a consequent loss of quality, it was an easier process than copper-plate engraving and consequently was widely practised – helping to reduce considerably the cost of illustrations in periodicals.

The 1870s, however, saw a revolution in printing. The photo-process made possible facsimile reproduction straight from the drawing. No longer did artists have to copy every single line of their picture or be subject to the engraver's personal interpretation. Now their drawings could be faithfully reproduced. This gave

them more freedom and reduced the price of printing, opening the way for cheaper publications.

Enterprising Victorian publisher James Henderson swiftly took advantage of this. Henderson was a genial, red-haired Scot, the shrewd publisher of the first halfpenny evening newspaper, **The Glasgow Evening Mercury** and the first penny daily paper, **The Glasgow Daily News**. When these were sufficiently established in the north, he expanded south, via Leeds and Manchester, to Red Lion Square, off Fleet Street.

Henderson's first London publication was **Our Young Folk's Weekly Budget** (2 January 1871). Throughout its twenty-five year life there were several title changes, although everyone knew it as **Young Folks**. The weekly bears the distinction of being the first to publish the classic story *Treasure Island*, with a serialization that started in the 1 October 1881 issue.

On 12 December 1874 Henderson issued **Funny Folks**, a weekly that was an important step on the evolutionary ladder of publishing.

Positioned between titles such as **Punch** and its imitators, and the later **Comic Cuts, Funny Folks** has been hailed as the first British comic. Well-produced on good quality paper, it published both the amusing written word and cartoons, many reprinted from American publications, and some original, although only occasionally were these sequential and therefore true comic strips. The front page always

featured one large cartoon, usually political, and was for many years drawn by the excellent John Stafford (1851-99).

Funny Folks was a tabloid for adults, declaring itself 'A Weekly Budget of Funny Pictures, Funny Notes, Funny Jokes, Funny Stories' and later, 'The Comic Companion to the Newspaper'. A few years later, Henderson launched **Scraps** (7 September 1883) and **Snap-Shots** (28 July 1890). Both were successful, established mainly on the basis of foreign reprints. **Scraps** ran for nearly seven years, **Snap-Shots** for almost ten.

In 1873, the year before **Funny Folks** was published, the magazine **Judy** issued a reprint collection of the *Ally Sloper* comic strips that had been appearing in the magazine since 1867. Priced at one shilling and enti-

tled *Ally Sloper, A Moral Lesson*, it was the world's first comic book. Several other reprint booklets were issued in the 1870s with art by Charles Ross and his wife Marie Duval. Ross later sold the rights to the character to his publisher, the engraver Gilbert Dalziel, who started a new paper called **Ally Sloper's Half Holiday** (3 May 1884) which became one of the most popular comics of the late Victorian era.

Dalziel initially hired American-born W.G. Baxter to draw the character which he did in superb style for the next three years. He then left and was replaced by the equally excellent W.F. Thomas, an expert draftsman and one of the leading comic artists of his day. The paper lasted 1570 issues, until 30 May 1914.

James Henderson's **Scraps** *ran for nearly seven years; here it celebrates Saint Patrick's Day, 1887*

Ally Sloper's Half Holiday *for 12 December 1885. The Sloper cartoon is by William Giles Baxter*

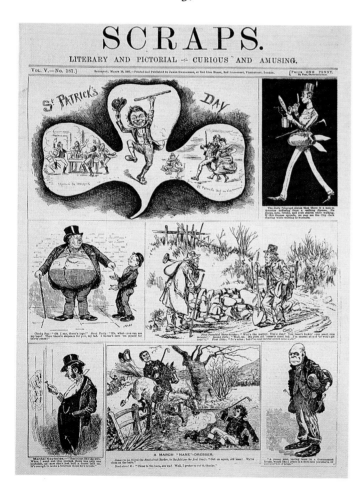

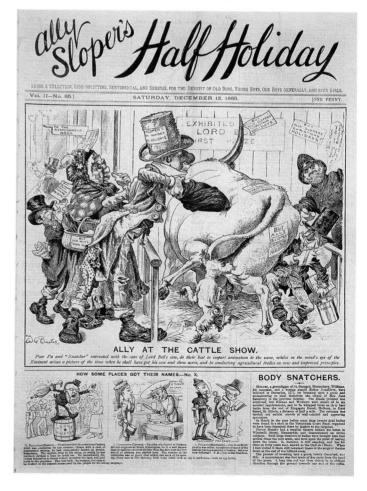

The Harmsworth revolution

Comic Cuts (1890) was easily recognizable as a comic; and in later years its proprietor, Alfred Harmsworth, was to boast that it was the first such publication. It was certainly the first to be priced at a halfpenny, which undercut his rivals by fifty per cent. Yet that was not the only reason for its success: Harmsworth was a publishing genius whose 'Midas touch' invariably gave people what they wanted at the right time. The touch rarely failed him, and it was with good reason that he was called the 'Napoleon of the Press'.

Alfred Charles William Harmsworth was born in Dublin in 1865, the son of a schoolmaster, later turned barrister. Two years later the family moved to London where Alfred grew up. He acquired an early taste for journalism, founding, editing and contributing to his school magazine.

After school he gained success as a freelance journalist. In the early 1880s he was writing articles and stories for various publications, which included James Henderson's **Young Folk's Tales** and Scraps. Still freelancing, he accepted a staff position on the paper **Youth** and then took an editorial post on **Bicycling News**, a Coventry-based publication. The year was 1886 and, brimming with ideas and energy, he approached publisher William Iliffe with a view to interesting him in a popular weekly based simply on readers' letters and replies to the same. The title he had in mind was **Answers to Correspondents**.

The concept was not strictly original: Harmsworth himself started a similar feature in his school magazine; and publisher George Newnes, who issued **Tit-Bits**, also made a feature of readers' letters in his publication. The novelty of Harmsworth's idea was that, in this case, letters would be the only feature.

Neither Iliffe nor Henderson expressed interest, though the latter advised Harmsworth that the title was too long. 'The public will simply call it **Answers**,' he declared — prophetically, as it turned out.

As a result, Harmsworth and some business partners set up their own company and, in June 1888, **Answers** was launched. By 1890 it was an established success and he was ready to expand.

His first move was to launch **Comic Cuts** (17 May 1890), the first halfpenny comic paper or, as Harmsworth put it on his now famous masthead: 'One Hundred Laughs for One Half Penny'. The price gave **Comic Cuts** an immediate advantage, and circulation rocketed. Within two years the new weekly was making more money

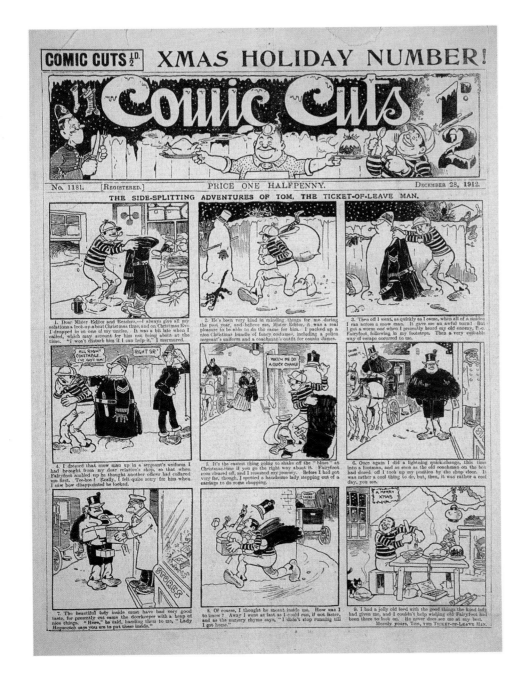

Comic Cuts *ran for sixty-three years. This front page features ex-convict* Tom, The Ticket-of-Leave Man*, drawn by Percy Cocking*

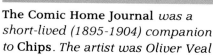

The Comic Home Journal was a short-lived (1895-1904) companion to Chips. *The artist was Oliver Veal*

Illustrated Chips *ran for sixty-three years before being axed by The Amalgamated Press in 1953. This front page features Weary Willie and Tired Tim who appeared every week for fifty-seven years*

than **Answers**. **Comic Cuts** was to last more that sixty years and become an English institution.

Less than three months later, on 26 July 1890, Harmsworth issued a companion: **Illustrated Chips** (**Chips** for short). This time he tried a sixteen-page half-tabloid format. It failed to sell, so after six weeks he converted it to a more acceptable full tabloid size and relaunched it from Number 1. This time it worked, circulation quickly matching that of **Comic Cuts**.

Alfred Harmsworth did not merely start the comic boom by introducing the half-price weekly; he was also one of the first to include original art in his publications. At first he reprinted material from **Puck**, **Judge**

and **Life** as Henderson had done. But soon advertisements appeared in **Comic Cuts** asking artists to submit drawings for publication. It was a turning point, encouraging many new talents to enter the field.

One of the artists who replied to Harmsworth's advertisements was Tom Browne (1870-1910). Browne's first work appeared in **Comic Cuts** under his *nom-de-plume* Vandyke Browne but his most famous creations were a pair of tramps who first appeared in **Chips** on 16 May 1896: *Weary Waddles and Tired Timmy*. They evolved into *Weary Willie and Tired Tim*, a fat and thin man team that appeared on the front page of **Chips** for an incredible fifty-seven years. **Chips** proved successful enough for Harmsworth later to launch **The Comic Home Journal** (11 May 1895) and publicize it as ' **The Friday Edition of Chips**'. It ran for 488 issues.

Alfred Harmsworth and his brothers (who were quickly brought on board as the business flourished) added a third weekly title to their production line with **The Wonder** (30 July 1892), a huge broadsheet which he converted to **Comic Cuts** size after twenty-seven issues. He renumbered it from No. 1 and changed the name to **The Funny Wonder**. It was another big success and although in subsequent years there were variations on the title, and more renumbering took place, essentially it was a weekly that had come to stay. Together with **Comic Cuts** and **Chips** it lasted until the three were axed, halfway through the next century, on 12 September 1953.

The halfpenny bandwagon

Meanwhile, Harmsworth's rivals had not been idle. Scarcely three months had elapsed when a halfpenny rival to **Comic Cuts** emerged. Would-be publishing entrepreneurs George Trapps and George Holmes formed a company and issued **Funny Cuts** on 12 July 1890, a weekly that would run for twenty years. Trapps Holmes & Company later issued **The World's Comic** (6 July 1892) and followed it with **Side Splitters** (6 August 1894). Both contained many jokes and some strips. **The World's Comic** ran for sixteen years but **Side Splitters** was not so fortunate: it was amalgamated with the former after just nine weeks. A better result was achieved by the firm's **Halfpenny Comic** (22 January 1898) which ran until 1906.

James Henderson issued the **Comic Pictorial Sheet** (29 September 1891), a broadsheet of jokes and cartoons reprinted from American magazines, and followed it with the similar, though smaller-format, **Comic Pictorial Nuggets** (7 May 1892). This was later simplified to **Nuggets** (26 November). The following year Henderson's Red Lion Square offices published **Varieties** (20 February 1893), a compilation of both original and reprint cartoons — this title being replaced by **The Garland** on 1 August 1896. Two years after that he launched his best selling title — **Pictorial Comic Life** (14 May 1898); later this became simply **Comic Life**.

Gilbert Dalziel, pleased with his success in launching **Ally Sloper's Half Holiday**, issued his second comic weekly, **Larks!**, on 1 May 1893. Like

Examples of Trapps Holmes's **Halfpenny Comic** *and* **Funny Cuts**. *The contents were inferior to those in Amalgamated Press titles*

the **Half Holiday**, it was well printed on better quality paper than its half-penny rivals. Its most famous regular characters were *The Balls Pond Banditti*, a gang of street urchins drawn by George Gordon Fraser. The weekly was taken over by Trapps Holmes from 9 December 1895.

Several other small publishers leaped on to the halfpenny comic bandwagon, although not all of them were successful. **Skits**, issued by the British Publishing Company on 27 June 1891, failed after only

twenty-three weeks. Charles Fox, a publisher of 'Penny Dreadfuls' (lurid tales sold in penny parts) did a great deal worse with his **Jolly Bits** (8 August 1892). This venture lasted a mere six weeks.

T. Murray Ford had better luck with **The Joker** on 18 July 1891, an eight-page halfpenny weekly printed on pink paper, and the firm issued a second title, **The Champion Comic**, on 9 January 1894. Both titles were still running at the end of 1895 but in January of the following year the

imprint became that of Greyfriars, and the two were amalgamated. Greyfriars later revamped **The Joker** and restarted the series from Number 1 as **The New Joker**. The page count was increased to twenty-four, and the price (now a penny) remained the same, but it was not enough: it failed after eleven weeks.

Another successful, if minor, entrant to the comic market was Cyril Arthur Pearson who issued **The Big Budget** on 19 June 1897. Some years before, in 1884, Pearson had entered a contest run by George Newnes in his weekly **Tit-Bits**. The prize was a job in the Newnes offices and it gave Pearson a start in a career in journalism. After six years he left Newnes and started his own company. Pearson's first publication was his version of Newnes's **Tit-Bits** and Harmsworth's **Answers**; he called it **Pearson's Weekly**, distinctive in its pink cover alongside the green **Tit-Bits** and orange **Answers**. Later, following the lead of Harmsworth (who launched the **Daily Mail** in 1897), Pearson ventured into newspaper publishing; he started the **Daily Express** in 1900.

The Big Budget comprised three sections and as such it was billed as 'Three Papers for One Penny'. Initially it published some fine original strips by top artists (Tom Browne, Jack Yeats, Tom Wilkinson) but later surrendered to US reprints (*The Katzenjammer Kids, Happy Hooligan*, and so on). By 1905 strips had disappeared and it became a boys' story paper. The editor was Alfred Brooke and the art editor 'Yorick' (Ralph Hodgson).

James Henderson's **Comic Life** *(1898-1928) was blessed with the superb talents of Harry O'Neill, here experimenting with picture formats in a* Tall Thomas and Butterball *adventure*

Comics in colour

Colour came to British comics on 12 September 1896. Once again it was the pioneering Alfred Harmsworth who led the advance with his 'Special Art Number' of **Comic Cuts**, a trial attempt at producing an all-colour weekly for a halfpenny. But there was the snag: colour doubled the price to a penny. However, Harmsworth kept on trying and, in the next few years, produced several other splendid coloured numbers of his three flagship weeklies. Each attempt was better than the last as his printers improved on their techniques and the process became cheaper. His aim was to produce each issue of a comic in full colour every week.

Alas, Harmsworth lost the race to his small rival, Trapps Holmes & Company. And not only did his competitors issue the first regular weekly comic to be printed in full colour, but they managed to do it for the same price as **Comic Cuts**: a halfpenny. Appropriately named **The Coloured Comic** (21 May 1898), it was a limited success: the full-colour printing continued for less than eighteen months before it was decided to print in one colour ink (blue) in order to justify the title.

Trapps Holmes & Company attempted special coloured numbers of their other titles too: at least two in 1898, including a special Fireworks Number. So did C. Arthur Pearson with colour editions of his **Big Budget** in 1903 and 1904. But once again it was Harmsworth's company that was responsible for the first regular comic to be printed in colour and to remain so.

He accomplished that with **Puck**, launched on 30 July 1904, and printed in full colour on the front, back and centrespread. It sounded like — and probably was — a steal of the US title, although the similarity ended there: its masthead boldly

*The up-market **Puck** was launched in 1904 and ran until the war cut off its paper supply in 1940. This superb front page was drawn by Harry O'Neill*

declared it was 'The Greatest Novelty of 1904'. But Harmsworth was at last forced to concede that it could not be produced for a halfpenny; the price was a penny and thereafter it remained the rule that colour comics would be priced at double their black-and-white counterparts.

Throughout the 1890s Harmsworth had initiated new comics and story-papers. For many of these he had started up new publishing companies and, in 1901, brought them together to form a new company, The Amalgamated Press. **Puck** was one of the earliest publications of Amalgamated Press (or AP). Much better than the earlier Trapps Holmes effort, it contained more colour and the strips had a quality indicative of better editorial control.

Colour comics became a regular event after the turn of the century. James Henderson launched his first colour weekly, **Lot-O-Fun**, on 17 March 1906 and followed it over the next few years by introducing colour to his existing titles: **Comic Life** (from 25 September 1909); **The Merry Thought & Scraps** (from 7 May 1910) and **Sparks** (from October 1918). The Amalgamated

Marvellous icicle imagery with Ragtime Rex *in this front page of The Amalgamated Press's* **The Favorite Comic**

The Rainbow, *The Amalgamated Press's famous weekly for young children: front-page star Tiger Tim was drawn by Herbert Foxwell*

Press followed its success with **Puck** by introducing colour to several subsequent new titles: **Chuckles** (10 January 1914), **The Rainbow** (14 January 1914), **Tiger Tim's Weekly** (19 November 1921) and **Jungle Jinks** (8 December 1923).

Yet something else had been happening to comics besides the advent of colour. Initially for adults, they began to be targeted at a much younger age group: children. The trend began with the introduction of a children's section within **Puck** called **Puck Junior**, and quickly spread to the whole comic.

This gathered pace and very soon all comics were being created for children. For the next half-century, that was the way it would remain.

Several 'black' comics were issued in the period leading up to World War 1. Henderson launched **The Big Comic** (17 January 1914); Trapps Holmes **Smiles** (5 May 1906) and **Picture Fun** (16 February 1909); and Amalgamated Press **The Butterfly** (17 September 1904), **Merry & Bright** (20 October 1910), **The Favorite Comic** (7 January 1911) and **The Firefly** (28 February 1914).

More 'ice-times' are had by side-splitter music-hall comedian Curly Kelly in this Amalgamated Press weekly, drawn by G.M. Payne

His name borrowed from part of English geography, Portland Bill *was the front-page star of* Butterfly *for twenty years, drawn mostly by G.M. Payne*

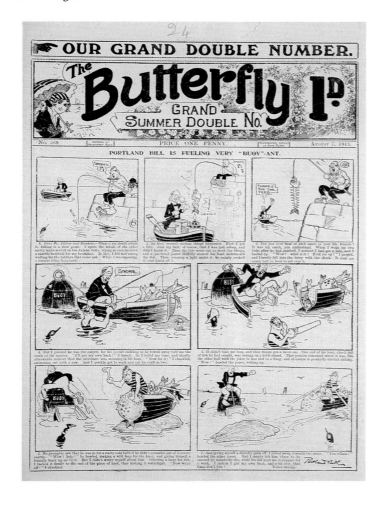

The Amalgamated Press, with the best pay rates, attracted the best artists; among them were Percy Cocking (who had taken over *Weary Willy and Tired Tim* on the front page of **Chips**), Albert ('Bertie') Brown (a prolific penman and the man behind the adventures of new film star Charlie Chaplin on the front page of **The Funny Wonder**) and Alex Akerbladh, a popular front-page artist who drew a myriad of strips. Illustrators whose careers began with Henderson soon moved to the Amalgamated Press once they had better developed their talents. In any event, the days of Harmsworth's rivals were numbered.

In 1920 the AP bought out the publications of both James Henderson and Trapps Holmes & Company. Weeklies issued by the latter were killed off: the still-running **Funny Cuts** and **Picture Fun** were far inferior to the classier AP productions. However, Henderson's weeklies **Comic Life**, **Lot-o'-Fun** and **Sparks** were worthy enough to enjoy an extended life under the AP imprint.

James Henderson's **The Big Comic** *was a weekly — and worthy — rival to The Amalgamated Press halfpenny comics*

Another top Henderson title was **Lot-o'-Fun** *which on its front page featured the adventures of* Dreamy Daniel *drawn by excellent penman George Davies*

Into the nursery

A baby boom followed the First World War. The AP quickly matched it with a boom of its own — in nursery comics. Nearly a dozen titles were issued during the Twenties, among them **The Children's Fairy** (1 November 1919), **Chicks' Own** (25 September 1920), **Bubbles** (16 April 1921), **Sunbeam** (7 October 1922), **Jungle Jinks** (8 December 1923), **Tiny Tots** (22 October 1927) and **Bo-Peep** (19 October 1929). Many of them lasted until the next war and, in some cases, even longer.

For decades the star of the nursery was *Tiger Tim* who, together with his pals the *Bruin Boys*, appeared in the popular titles **Tiger Tim's Weekly** and **The Rainbow**.

Tiger Tim was an anthropomorphized beast whose first appearance was in a **Daily Mirror** one-shot comic strip on 16 April 1904, drawn by talented Julius Stafford Baker.

In November 1904 Baker was commissioned to draw *Tiger Tim* on a regular basis for **The Monthly Playbox**, the children's supplement to the magazine **The World and his Wife**. There the feature remained popular for some years. Julius Baker also drew *Tim* and his pals for **The Playbox Annual** which started in 1909. So he was the natural choice to draw *Tim* and the *Bruin Boys* for the front page of AP's new weekly, **The Rainbow**, when it was launched on 14 February 1914. But soon other artists took over, first S.J. Cash, then Herbert Foxwell (1890-1943).

Foxwell was a natural when it came to drawing comic animals. Baker had drawn the animals spindly and beastlike. Foxwell took the opposite approach: his pen endowed *Tim* and his pals with a full-bodied look, fleshing them out to human proportions. This made them more attractive, adding to their popularity and so to their success.

Bubbles was a weekly for nursery-age children. Notice the superb title art

There is no mistaking the age group for this long-running weekly which claimed to help children to read by hyphenating words

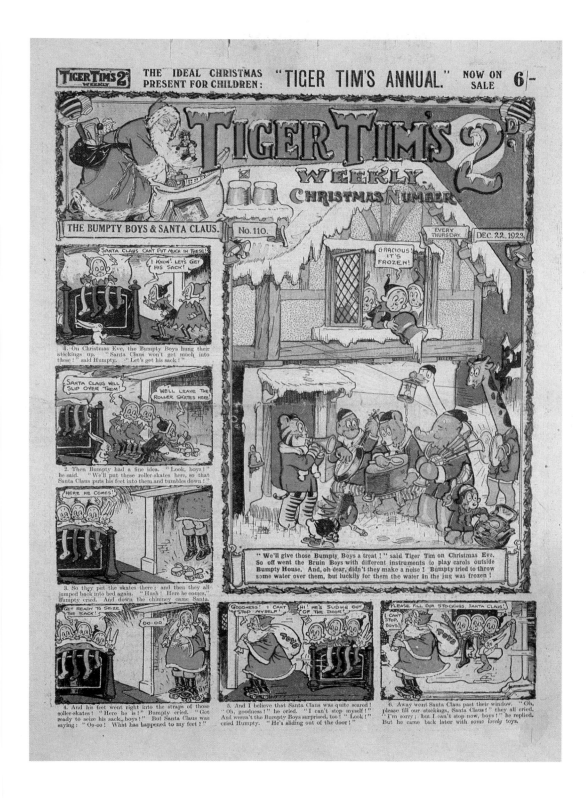

*Following an enthusiastic reception in **The Rainbow**, The Amalgamated Press gave front-page star Tiger Tim his own weekly which ran from 1920 to 1940. The artist was Herbert Foxwell. The Bumpty Boys were drawn by Fred Crompton*

The Rainbow became one of the AP's best-selling weeklies.

Herbert Foxwell served in the army during the First World War, earning a promotion to captain. Although his time was necessarily limited, he still managed to be a consistent contributor to AP weeklies. After the

armistice in 1918, with paper restrictions eased, new titles started to appear regularly. **The Rainbow** was followed by **Tiger Tim's Tales** (1 June 1919), which was soon relaunched as **Tiger Tim's Weekly** (31 January 1920).

With more free time, Foxwell's out-

put was prolific; his work also matured, earning him a reputation as premier artist of the nursery comics. *Tim* and the *Bruin Boys* became Twenties super-stars: by the end of the decade Herbert Foxwell's *Tiger Tim* was featured in no less than six publications. In addition, Foxwell drew female counterparts, *Tiger*

A companion to **Tiny Tots**, *the nursery comic* **Sunbeam** *was published by The Amalgamated Press from 1922 to 1940*

Chuckles *was issued by The Amalgamated Press in 1914. The front page artist was the accomplished Tom Wilkinson*

Tilly and the *Hippo Girls*, for **The Playbox** and its corresponding annual, the latter title a new weekly started on 14 February 1925.

Another leading nursery comic was **Chicks' Own** (25 September 1920), a weekly popular with parents because it claimed to teach children to read by hyphenating all its words. Front page star for almost the entire thirty-seven year run was *Rupert the Chick*, drawn for just as long by veteran Arthur White.

Chicks' Own, **Sunbeam** (7 October 1922) and **Tiny Tots** (22 October 1927) were all controlled by Langton Townley, one of the most successful of the AP editors, who joined Harmsworth Brothers in the very early years. **Tiny Tots**, too, used hyphenated words and enjoyed a long run up until 1959, while **Sunbeam** lasted for eighteen years, until 1940.

Not all nursery weeklies, however, enjoyed long runs. **Jungle Jinks** (8 December 1923) was abandoned after only sixty-two issues. It replaced **Chuckles** (10 January 1914), a well-produced weekly with pleasing use of colour. The front pages of both comics were drawn by the excellent Tom Wilkinson.

Chuckles was the only AP comic to be printed in colour and priced at a halfpenny — though not for long: wartime shortages soon sent the price zooming.

The now long-established **Puck** had its fine artists too. One of them was Walter Booth (1892-1971) who had previously worked for Henderson. Booth was asked to draw the first dramatic picture serial in British comics: *Rob the Rover*, which began in **Puck** on 15 May 1920. *Rob* featured the adventures of a young boy globe-trotter. Beautifully drawn, in large black-and-white pictures, it ran for twenty years until the war brought it to an end in 1940.

Fun from films

Other things were happening in the 1920s besides nursery comics. On 17 January 1920 AP issued Number 1 of one of the most successful British comics ever produced: **Film Fun**. This half-tabloid-size weekly, sans colour, featured the stars of the silent cinema, and later the talkies, in one- or two-page picture strips.

The idea was not new. Celebrities had appeared in the comics for years; ever since popular music-hall comedian Dan Leno featured in his own weekly, **Dan Leno's Comic Journal** (26 February 1898), stage luminaries had appeared in various titles. The AP ventured into films when it put Charlie Chaplin on the front page of **The Funny Wonder** in 1915. Definitively drawn by Bertie Brown, it was hugely popular and lasted for nearly thirty years. Giving film stars their own comic weekly was a natural extension of all this.

Film Fun took off like a rocket! Riding high on the immense popularity of the two-reeler comedy shorts, it quickly established a big circulation. And in true Harmsworth/AP 'eliminate the competition before it starts' style, a companion weekly was issued on 24 April 1920: **The Kinema Comic**. It left little scope for other publishers: **Film Fun** featured the most popular stars, **The Kinema** most of those remaining. Because of that, perhaps, and a title that dated quickly, **Kinema's** run was shorter: it lasted until 15 October 1932 whereas **Film Fun** lasted for forty-two years, until 15 September 1962.

In the Thirties another film comic was launched: **Film Picture Stories** (28 July 1934). Where **Film Fun** and **Kinema** focused on humour, **Film Picture Stories** was the first to feature all dramatic films in picture strip form. But comedy was still king; **Film Picture Stories** failed after thirty weeks. All three comics were edited by Fred Cordwell (1886-

1948). An extrovert who mixed panache and vulgarity in equal proportion, he had earlier worked on other AP weeklies **Merry & Bright**, **Firefly** and **Butterfly**. While there Cordwell had commissioned work from one artist in particular: George William Wakefield (1887-1942).

Cordwell had observed not only that Wakefield was an excellent artist but also that he was adept at captur-

Early film funnymen were a big hit and editors quickly capitalized on their popularity: Artist Bertie Brown drew a definitive Charlie Chaplin

In 1920 The Amalgamated Press issued two weeklies packed with movie stars. First came **Film Fun** *[see next page], then hard on its heels came* **The Kinema Comic** *[right]. Harry Langdon is drawn by George Wakefield*

ing the human likeness. This made him perfectly suited to **Film Fun**; so much so that Cordwell made him principal artist and based all three of his cinema weeklies on his style, instructing his other artists to draw as Wakefield did.

George Wakefield's best-known comic strip was *Laurel and Hardy*, which he drew for **Film Fun** from 1930; later it appeared on the front page for some twenty-three years. Like Brown's *Charlie Chaplin*, Wakefield's version of the comedy duo was definitive. After Wakefield's death, *Laurel and Hardy* was taken on by various artists; after the war ended, in 1945, his son Terry became the main artist until 1957 when the strip was discontinued after the death of Oliver Hardy.

Film Fun *[page 32] featured bespectacled genius* Harold Lloyd, *later followed by* Laurel and Hardy *who occupied the front and back pages for twenty-three years.*

SCREAMINGLY
:: FUNNY ::

COMIC DISGUISE INSIDE
ABSOLUTELY FREE.

THIS
COPY!

Film Fun 2ᵈ
our Grand Free Gift No

No. 254. Vol. 5.

November 22nd, 1924.

The Lively Larks of HAROLD LLOYD
The Pathé Mirth Merchant.

This Week: "IT REBOUNDED ON THAT BOUNDER!"

WHAT A MUDDY ROAD, HAROLD!

1. "Oh dear, Harold, how muddy the road is!" cried Gertie to our hearty, handsome, happy hero. And it was muddy, too, and no question. Now, there were three jolly old sandwich-men about to cross the road. So what did this fine fellow Harold do? Ah! Ho, what a lad he is!

2. Why, old Harold took several coins out of his pocket and slung them, with unerring aim, just in front of these cheery old guys, who promptly proceeded to bend so's to pick them up. And, of course, this was just what Harold wanted them to do. Right y'are, then! Splendid!

OVER YOU GO, GERTIE!

MONEY!

3. As I say, down went the good old advertising experts, and Harold remarked: "That's the caper! Over you go, Gertie!" And over went Gertie, across the old boards, thereby keeping her shoes nice and clean. And how's that for an idea, eh? Don'tcher think that Harold's the limit?

4. Any old how, the sandwich-men picked up the coins, and Harold and Gertie reached the pavement on the other side of the road all cheerio. And that, my old dears, is the finish of EPISODE I. Now then we come to EPISODE II. Now for the thrill. Now for the business. (Continued on page 24.)

The Golden Age

From the late Twenties to the early Thirties about a dozen new titles were launched by the Amalgamated Press. These mostly added to, rather than replaced, existing weeklies. By this time all comics were for children and the characters and the humour of the strips reflected this: the majority were aimed at seven- to eleven-year-olds.

'Penny Blacks' included **Larks** (29 October 1927), **Jingles** (13 January 1934), **Tip Top** (21 April 1934), **Jolly** (19 January 1935) and **Golden** (23 October 1937). Twopenny Coloureds were **My Favourite** (28 January 1928), **Crackers** (28 February 1929), **Bo-Peep** (19 October 1929) and, at the apex of what was later accepted as a Golden Age of British Comics, there was **Happy Days** (8 October 1938), a resplendent photogravure publication, the front page of which was drawn by Roy Wilson.

There were many good artists working for AP comics in the 1930s, although only a small number provided most of the artwork. The majority of these were freelance artists and of them all Roy Wilson was the accepted dean: the most influential artist of the Golden Age.

Roy Wilson began his career just after the First World War following a chance meeting in a pub with a man named Don Newhouse, an established comic artist who had worked for Henderson. Wilson was assistant to Newhouse throughout the Twenties but by the early Thirties had branched out on his own. In a few years he was the AP's top artist, supplying front page artwork for their most popular weeklies.

Wilson's best work was for the Christmas week numbers of late 1930s humour comics. It culminated in the short-lived weekly **Happy Days**, for which he drew an

Jingles: *issued by Amalgamated Press; front page by Roy Wilson*

Tip Top: *issued by Amalgamated Press; front page by Roy Wilson*

My Favourite: *issued by Amalgamated Press; front page by George Wakefield*

The Jolly Comic: *issued by Amalgamated Press; front page by Bertie Brown*

Crackers: *issued by Amalgamated Press; front page by Reg Parlett*

animal strip called *Chimpo's Circus*. Although he illustrated for the comics until his death in 1965, owing to the war and the slump that followed, it was never again possible to show off his work at its very best.

Happy Days was the AP's response to **Mickey Mouse Weekly** (8 February 1936), a tabloid comic that was the first to use the photogravure process. Issued by Willbank Publications, it featured all the main Disney characters and included new indigenous material as well. The front page was a single picture of *Mickey* and friends, often indulging

Expensive photogravure reproduction and Roy Wilson's artistry made **Happy Days** *most attractive but there were only forty-five issues: it is now much sought after by collectors*

in the very English customs of the Boat Race and Guy Fawkes celebrations. It was splendidly drawn by Wilfred Haughton.

Inside, the US reprint material appeared alongside British humorous strips such as *Skit, Skat and the Captain* (Basil Reynolds), the science-fiction serial *Ian on Mu* (Stanley White) and historical dramas *Road to Rome* and *Sons of the Sword*, drafted by the superb Reg Perrott. **Mickey Mouse Weekly** was one of the most successful of all British comics: it ran for twenty-one years until 28 December 1957. It proved that the mighty Amalgamated Press was not impregnable on this front.

Another of the AP's competitors in the 30s, though to a lesser extent, was Target Publications of Bath which published several titles from its provincial West Country headquarters: **Rattler** (19 August 1933), **Dazzler** (19 August 1933), **Chuckler** (31 March 1934), **Target** (15 June 1935), **Rocket** (26 October 1935) and **Bouncer** (11 February 1939).

Some of these titles also included the free promotional comic **Ovaltiney's Own** (1935-1938). And, despite the generally low standard of artwork, it meant no small success for this small publisher daring to compete with the AP in its own market. Too much success, evidently, for in 1939 the larger firm bought them out and eventually all of the Target titles disappeared.

Triumph *from Amalgamated Press reprinted early* Superman *adventures. The British cover artist was John McCaill*

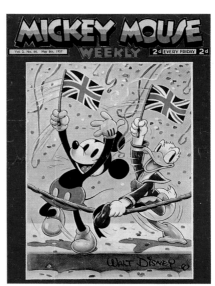

A unique picture on the front page of **Mickey Mouse Weekly**, *published by Odhams: two of the most famous US comic characters celebrate a very British event — the Coronation of Edward VIII — with a wave of their Union Jacks!*

The new entertainment medium in the 1930s was the radio and, wishing to emulate their success with **Film Fun**, *The Amalgamated Press started* **Radio Fun**, *a weekly that proved to be equally popular. The artist here was Reg Parlett, who had a seventy-year career in comics*

Vintage titles from Dundee include Dandy *still running fifty years on. This front page: James Crighton © D.C. Thompson & Co Ltd*

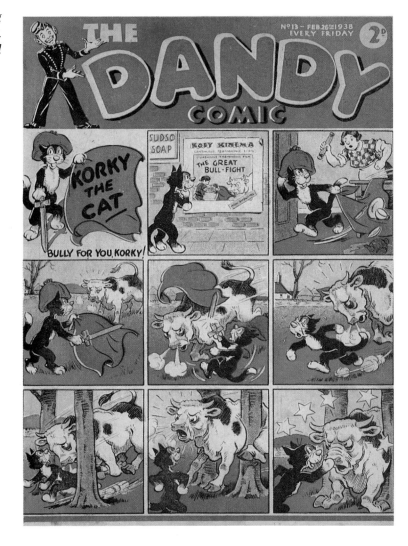

Not all competitors, however, could be dealt with so easily. A Scottish publisher, D.C. Thomson, with headquarters in Dundee, owned two newspapers and, in the Twenties, had started a line of story papers for boys. These were **Rover**, **Wizard**, **Adventure**, **Hotspur** and **Skipper**, collectively known as 'The Big Five'. Thomson was a hugely successful firm run by hard-nosed businessmen who understood what they were about.

On 4 December 1937, D.C. Thomson launched **The Dandy Comic**, an irreverent, jaunty newcomer to the children's market that would have repercussions for decades to come. It was half-tabloid with a full-colour front page and made no concessions to purchasing parents: it aimed directly at kids. Big stars were *Korky the Cat* and *Desperate Dan*, who are still running in the same title fifty-five years on.

D.C. Thomson issued two similar weeklies before the Second World War decimated the publishing industry: **The Beano Comic** (30 July 1938) and **The Magic Comic** (22 July 1939). The **Beano** is also still running, as is one of its original strips, *Lord Snooty*. The **Magic**, aimed at very young children, died after a run of eighty weeks.

The Amalgamated Press made a quick but initially confused response with two half-tabloids, each having a colour front page – any resemblance to **The Dandy** being no coincidence! The first was **Radio Fun** (15 October 1938), a weekly that had the splendid idea of featuring radio stars – except that the front-page star was *George*, a carthorse drawn by Roy Wilson which did not have the slightest connection with anything that was being broadcast!

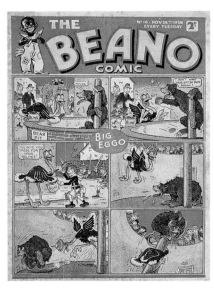

Like **Dandy***, the* **Beano** *has also passed its fiftieth birthday © D.C. Thompson & Co Ltd*

The Magic Comic *was discontinued in 1941. This front page: E.H. Banger © D.C. Thompson & Co Ltd*

AP followed through with the hopefully named **Knock-Out Comic** (4 March 1939), a weekly that traded more in knockabout fun than in the radio. Why then was the front-page strip called *Our Crazy Broadcasters* a wireless comedy act? It was because the initial idea of one comic had been made into two by the controlling editor. But within weeks it had all been sorted out: radio star Arthur Askey (drawn by Reg Parlett) replaced George on the front of **Radio Fun** and *Deed-a-Day Danny* (by Hugh McNeill) began a long run on page one of **Knock-Out**.

Paper rationing and a general shortage of supplies killed off many comics during the Second World War. Another problem was that artists and publishing staff were called up, not to return for the duration. Those comics that were left were reduced to fewer pages and fortnightly publication. The war proved a grim time for British comics.

Yet in the face of all that, enterprising publisher Gerald Swan, a former street market trader, managed to obtain a quota of paper and, boosted by stock he had accumulated in warehouses around London, supplied much of the capital's reading throughout the war.

Swan based his output on the new type of American comic book that had begun to reach England in the late 1930s. Reprint titles like **Famous Funnies** and monthlies such as **New Fun** — which featured original material — had proved extremely popular on his market stall. So, when the supplies from the USA drew to a halt, Swan decided to start publishing his own American-style comic books, printed in black-and-white.

Emulating the titles of the new US publications, in 1940 he launched seven new titles in rapid succession: **New Funnies** (February), **Topical Funnies** (April), **Thrill Comics**

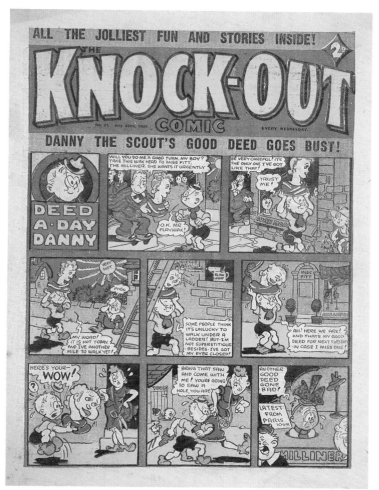

*The **Knock-Out Comic** was first issued by The Amalgamated Press on 4 March 1939. This early issue features* Deed-a-Day Danny

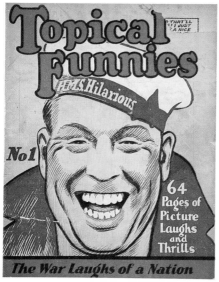

English comics in US format were issued by British publisher Gerald G. Swan. **Topical Funnies**, *April 1940: cover art by John Woods*

(April), **War Comics** (May), **Slick Fun** (June), **Fresh Fun** (June) and **Extra Fun** (July). All had a generally low standard of artwork: although not dramatically inferior to the standard of the American drawing, it looked rather worse due to the lack of colour. But there were some notable exceptions; moonlighting AP artists Don Newhouse, Frank Minnitt, Percy Cocking and Wally Robertson made contributions which raised the tone.

The work of one ex-AP artist in particular became a permanent feature. Edward Henry Banger (pronounced to rhyme with 'ranger': 1897-1968) was responsible for the Swan housestyle. Banger was an excellent draftsman and the epitome of British comic tradition. His work was the mainstay of the Swan comics as long as they lasted, until the late Fifties.

After the war ended in 1945, paper restrictions remained in force until around 1950. The AP and its rival, D.C. Thomson, slowly returned their publications to a weekly schedule but were unable to launch new comics for some time. The gap was filled by a number of small publishers who issued scores of titles. Many were one-shots; all of them had short runs. By the early Fifties all supply restrictions had been lifted and the publishing industry returned to full production. It finished for good the output of these enterprising publishers; but while they lasted they were an interesting and colourful addition to news-stands.

Some of the short-run comics issued by small publishers in the post-war years

Enter the *Eagle*

A major landmark of British comics publishing was **Eagle**, which appeared on 14 April 1950. The publisher was Hulton Press which issued the prestigious national weekly **Picture Post** and other quality magazines. The firm had never previously published a comic but had been persuaded to do so by a clergyman from Preston, the Reverend Marcus Morris.

Morris had encountered American horror comic imports and was appalled at their content. He had already 'dipped his toe' into publishing with **The Anvil**, a parish magazine that he was able to bring to national circulation. He decided to put together a weekly comic that would be morally pure and produced to the highest standard.

The Reverend's principal artist on **The Anvil** was a talented young man named Frank Hampson who was recruited to help design the new comic and to draw comic strips. Hampson created *Dan Dare – Pilot of the Future*, a superbly drawn, well scripted feature that appeared on the **Eagle**'s front page. Inside strips were also by Hampson, along with several other fine artists including Frank Humphris, John Ryan, Martin Aitchison and Richard Jennings.

Eagle was a huge success. In the early years its circulation topped a million. *Dan Dare*, however, was always the most popular strip and was mainly responsible for that success. Without the intrepid *Pilot of the Future*, it is doubtful that **Eagle** would have been so popular for so long. Morris and Hulton soon created companion papers: **Girl** (2 November 1951), **Robin** (28 March 1953), and **Swift** (20 March 1954) –

The high-flying **Eagle**, *issued by Hulton Press on 14 April 1950, was a major landmark for British comics, setting high standards and introducing* Dan Dare

Eagle *was later joined by companion weeklies,* **Girl** *and* **Swift***, the first issue of which appears above*

Lion *No. 1 (23 February 1952)*
featured Captain Condor

Tiger *No. 1 (11 September 1954)*
featured Roy of the Rovers

each cleverly designed to fit into particular niche markets.

Impressed, the Amalgamated Press launched its first post-war comic, **Lion** (23 February 1952), along the same lines. But although modelled on **Eagle**, it could never be said to be a competitor. **Lion** was half the size, non-photogravure and had colour on the front and back pages only. The page one star was *Captain*

Condor, like *Dan Dare*, a spaceman. Although he lacked the 'class' of *Dare*, *Condor* did have his attractions. He was more robust than his **Eagle** counterpart, as were the interior features in **Lion**.

Eagle was discontinued in 1969, long after Frank Hampson had left and it was ignominiously incorporated into its rival, **Lion**. That weekly lasted until 1974. *Captain Condor*

died with **Lion** but another popular picture strip featured *Robot Archie*, a mechanical man controlled by two men, Ted Richie and Ken Dale. *Robot Archie* has had an extended life in other titles right up to the present day. Initially drawn by Alan Philpott, the strip's best-known artist was Ted Keirnan.

Although never notching up the kind of circulation **Eagle** enjoyed, **Lion** did well enough for the AP to launch a companion, **Tiger** (11 September 1954). The front-page star here was more down to earth: a soccer player, *Roy Race*, who played for Melchester Rovers. Drawn for many years by the excellent Joe Colquhoun (1927-87), *Roy of the Rovers* outlasted **Tiger**. He was eventually given his own weekly which is still running today.

Eagle, **Lion** and **Tiger** were all boys' adventure comics. There were new 'funnies' weeklies too. D.C. Thomson's first post-war comic was **The Topper** (7 February 1953) followed by the similar **Beezer** (21 January 1956). Both were tabloid with colour on the front page and both introduced some classic characters.

The Topper featured *Beryl the Peril* (drawn by David Law) and *Mickey the Monkey* (by Dudley D. Watkins). **The Beezer** had *The Banana Bunch* (Leo Baxendale), *Pop, Dick and Harry* (Tom Bannister) and *Ginger* (Dudley Watkins). Both weeklies had strong support from one- and two-page strips by D.C. Thomson's best artists and were imaginative, lively additions to the news-stands.

Not quite so imaginative was the AP's new funnies title, **TV Fun** (19 September 1953) which had strips featuring television personalities. It was apt: the growth of the medium had stopped in the Forties but in the Fifties was expanding rapidly. Furthermore, television audiences appeared to be eating into the readership of comics.

The Topper *and* The Beezer, *two No.1 funnies titles from D.C. Thomson*
© *D.C. Thompson & Co Ltd*

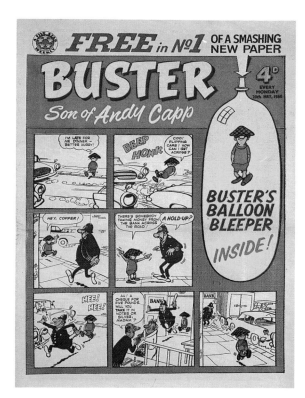

Buster No. 1, issued by Fleetway Publications on 28 May 1960, with art by Nadal. The title is still running

Baxendale and Reid

D.C. Thomson's **Beano** and **Dandy** returned to weekly production in 1949. Under the respective editorships of George Mooney and Albert Barnes, they were revitalized with new features and new artists. Foremost were Leo Baxendale and Ken Reid. Baxendale broke with British comics' tradition by introducing a new style and an anarchic slant in humour. His best work was on strips like *Minnie the Minx*, *Little Plum*, *The Three Bears* and *The Bash Street Kids*. Baxendale became the most talented and influential artist since Roy Wilson in the Thirties and his influence is still felt strongly today, forty years on.

Ken Reid was the creator of *Fudge the Elf*, a popular comic strip that he wrote and drew for the provincial newspaper, **Manchester Evening News**. His unique style of drawing and macabre sense of humour was seen at its best in *Roger the Dodger*, *Bing-Bang Benny* and *Angel Face*.

By 1960 the Amalgamated Press had ceased to exist. It was taken over by Cecil King's Mirror Group, publishers of the national newspaper, the **Daily Mirror**. King was a nephew of Alfred Harmsworth, the firm's creator, and hell-bent on the acquisition trail. He merged the AP with his Mirror Group and other purchases to create the International Publishing Corporation (IPC). result was that some of AP's best known titles were soon killed off, including **Film Fun**, **Knock-Out** and **Chicks' Own**. Others, **Comic Cuts**, **The (Funny) Wonder** and **Chips**, had died back in the early Fifties, their epitaph being that sixty-year-old titles were too old-fashioned for modern consumption.

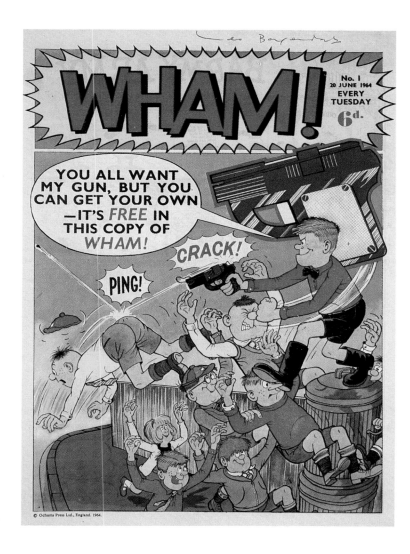

Wham! No. 1, issued by Odhams Press on 20 June 1964, with art by Leo Baxendale

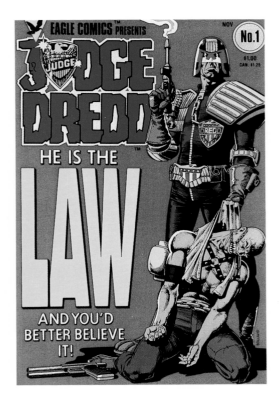

Sixteen years on Judge Dredd's adventures were reprinted in a widely available US comic book format. Cover by the best new-age British artist, Brian Bolland

2000 AD was an immediate success in 1977, its biggest star not the revitalized Dan Dare but Judge Dredd from the second issue

IPC's first comic (issued under the imprint of Fleetway Publications) was **Buster** (28 May 1960 and still running). **Buster** was also the name of the lead feature, *Buster, Son of Andy Capp)*. The connection with the **Daily Mirror** was being exploited to full advantage: *Andy Capp*, the famous newspaper strip with international circulation, had been created for the **Mirror**.

In 1964 Leo Baxendale broke away from D.C. Thomson and went to Odhams Press, a publisher with a long history but new to comics. Could Odhams take on its huge rivals and win? Well, why not? Hulton had been going for fourteen years before bringing out **Eagle**. The first Odhams weekly was **Wham!** (20 June 1964), printed in photogravure with several pages in full colour. The majority of its features were drawn by Baxendale, with some others by his ex-colleague from D.C. Thompson, Ken Reid.

Wham! — intended to be a progressive **Beano** — was successful enough to spawn a competitor, **Smash!** (5 February 1966). Both Odhams titles at first featured good quality, original British material, but it was not to last. In 1967 US reprints started to appear. Riding on the back of the popularity of the TV series was *Batman* and, later, reprints of the new Marvel superheroes. A third Odhams title, **Pow!** (21 January 1967), soon featured more US material than British.

Soon Odhams were publishing weeklies that were almost entirely reprints: **Fantastic** (10 February 1967) and **Terrific** (15 April 1967). But they were to have short lives: both died in the following year, as did **Wham!** and **Pow!** In keeping with British comics' tradition, they were merged prior to their demise (becoming **Fantastic and Terrific, Pow! and Wham!**, and the slightly over-the-top **Smash! and Pow! and Fantastic!**). When IPC took over Odhams in 1969 only **Smash!** was left. It continued until 1971.

The 1970s saw a new line in humour comics from IPC with an occasional foray into the market by D.C. Thomson. IPC's **Whizzer & Chips** (18 October 1969), **Cor!!** (6 June 1970), **Shiver & Shake** (10 March 1973), and **Whoopee!** (9 March 1974) were only the first of several such titles, many of which had short runs. All were half-tabloid with more aggressive humour than that of their earlier counterparts. However, unlike US funnies comics which had longer stories and therefore allowed better plot development, the British weeklies rarely featured anything that ran for more than two pages.

In 1977 IPC launched **2000 AD** which became the most successful British comic since **Eagle**. It had an innovative line in heroes — or antiheroes — and a high standard of writing and art. Like **Eagle** with *Dan Dare*, **2000 AD** also had a superstar: *Judge Dredd*, a lawman of the future whose right-wing philosophy in a post-nuclear society was exaggerated to truly comic proportions.

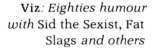

Viz*: Eighties humour
with* Sid the Sexist, Fat
Slags *and others*

Dredd was the creation of Pat Mills and John Wagner, both first-rate writers. A succession of talented artists, in particular Brian Bolland, have helped to keep the weekly popular for fifteen years. Its continued success will inevitably mean a change of title as the year itself approaches. Alan Moore was another writer to gain respect and recognition for his stories in the pages of **2000 AD**. Moore went on to pen tales for US comics, as did many of the other writers and artists whose work had appeared in **Science Fiction** weekly.

The biggest success story of the Eighties, however, was **Viz**, an adult comic founded in 1979 in the Newcastle home of Chris and Simon Donald. It has achieved a circulation of around a million with aggressively juvenile but often very funny one-page strips such as *Sid the Sexist* (subtitle: *tits out for the lads*) and similar.

Viz has spawned a clutch of imitators: **Poot!**, **Smut**, **Filth**, **Gas** and **Brain Damage**, to mention but a few, all of which contain even 'harder' material than **Viz** which, alongside them, can appear almost subtle. Perhaps publisher John Brown should have emulated his predecessor of a century before, Alfred Harmsworth. Once Harmsworth realized he had a hit, he went about creating his own competition, so squeezing other publishers out of the market. The present-day market for 'adult' comics at £1 a time is around 1.5 million every fortnight, plus lucrative advertising revenue.

This type of humour may be the latest fad in British comics — **Viz** is a crude, rude satirical version of the **Beano** — but neither the comic nor its clones are likely to last. The blend is too hard to maintain, as a forerunner, **Oink!** (a comic based on pigs!), discovered in the early Eighties.

For the most part British comics have never grown up. Whether they are aimed at children or adults, the humour remains essentially juvenile and the action adventure strips, with too few exceptions, lack maturity. In Britain, comics are published for kids (even if they are labelled 'adult'). Other nations have often progressed beyond this, which partly explains why material produced for the British market fails to travel well. Moreover, countless readers on the home front turn to imports to obtain what they want. British comics, therefore, do not prosper as they might.

This leads to some frustration, for the technicians — the writers and artists — are often first-rate. New ideas can be startlingly original and different perspectives abound on traditional themes thought to have been played out long ago. To see what can happen when British creators have access to a more mature market, one need look no further than writers and artists such as Alan Moore, Dave Gibbons, Brian Bolland and others who have made up the **2000 AD** contingent which has been so successful in its work for US comics.

So what is to be done? If the creative talent is there and the publishers are eager to profit (as they must be) from this most popular of media, perhaps it is the middle men, the editors, who lack training, expertise and vision. And the publishers could help more too! The pool of talent is small and needs to be nurtured. A system of creators' rights, with royalties and reprint fees, and work credits, would provide much-needed incentives: creating such a system could herald the dawn of a new Golden Age of British Comics.

VOLUME XXXV.   NEW YORK, FEBRUARY 8, 1900.   NUMBER 899.
Entered at the New York Post Office as Second-Class Mail Matter.
Copyright, 1900, by LIFE PUBLISHING COMPANY.

LIFE

AMERICANUS SUM

AMERICA'S TYPICA

NO. 24
JAN.-FEB.

The Mirth of a Nation

Arc

THE INCR

12¢

HUI

DC
PUBLICATION

NO. 1

MAR...APR.

DC
A SUPERMAN
PUBLICATION

SUPERBOY

Ten
Cents

E POWERFUL!
E DANGEROUS!
UNCONTROLLA
EVER BEFORE.
COMES THE H

DC

10¢

SHOWCASE

APPROVED
BY THE
COMICS
CODE
AUTHORITY

SUPERMAN
NATIONAL COMICS

Presents **SUPERMAN**'s **GIRL FRIEND**

LOIS LANE

BA

in

"MRS. SUPERMAN

ALSO:
"THE GIRL FROM

THANK GOODNESS
YOU'VE COME HOME,

AMERICAN COMICS

The earliest comics to appear in the USA were 'Picture Sheets' — single tabloid pages with up to twelve pictures on one side. There were no word-balloons, each picture having accompanying text beneath, and they were produced both in black-and-white and colour. The idea was imported by immigrants from Europe where such publications had been popular since the eighteenth century.

In the United States the earliest Picture Sheets were issued by the Humoristic Publishing Company, Kansas City, Missouri in 1888, although other Picture Sheets could well have been distributed before this in their native languages. During the latter half of the nineteenth century various other publications were issued which could lay claim to being direct ancestors of the American comic. These precursors included: **Scraps** (D.C. Johnston; Boston 1849); the English language version of Wilhelm Busch's **Max und Moritz** (1871); **Stuff and Nonsense** (1884) by A.B. Frost; **The Bull Calf and Other Tales** (1892). And, significantly, there were the humour magazines.

The three most popular and influential American cartoon magazines were **Puck**, **Judge** and **Life**. Again, the European influence was strong. The man responsible for **Puck** was Austrian-born Joseph Keppler (1837-94) who had arrived in the USA in the 1860s. Keppler's first publishing venture was the German language **Die Vehme**, to which he also contributed cartoons. It was short-lived but he tried again (twice) with **Puck**, still issued in German. But **Puck** only found real success when Keppler launched an English language edition on 14 March 1877.

During its forty-year run, the magazine, with its famous Shakespearean masthead legend 'What fools these mortals be!', featured the work of some of the finest cartoon-

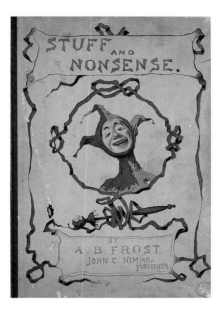

Precursor of modern comic books, **Stuff and Nonsense**, *a collection of A.B. Frost cartoons first published in* **Harper's Monthly**

The work of Charles Dana Gibson had a devastating impact on the front page of **Life** *as shown on this superb pre-Valentine issue [right]*

Puck, *started in 1877, was the first of the great American cartoon magazines*

VOLUME XXXV.   NEW YORK, FEBRUARY 8, 1900.   NUMBER 899.

LIFE

"Fairly Bristling with His Darts."
See verses, page 109.

this relatively recent innovation of the popular press in favour of powerful black-and-white illustrations. And no one was better at that — or more largely responsible for the great success of **Life** — than its star cartoonist — Charles Dana Gibson (1867-1944).

Gibson's penmanship and astute observation of the times in which he lived earned him a high reputation and made him one of the most acclaimed and famous cartoonists in America. Particularly popular were his depictions of sophisticated and beautiful young women. He created a look that became recognizable by millions as 'The Gibson Girl'. In 1920 Gibson became the owner and editor of **Life**. Later, however, the journal was sold and eventually became the world-famous photo-magazine.

Nevertheless, the most obvious starting point for US comics was in the 1880s. The frontiers of publishing were fast advancing. Improvements in printing made it easier to reproduce line drawings, and newspapers, keen to achieve an edge in the circulation battle, were quick to commission artists to brighten up their pages. At first their efforts were confined to news and features, but it was not long before cartoons began to appear.

The majority of the population was educated, literate and relatively affluent. Newspapers proliferated and circulations grew. A number of daily papers started to publish an extra edition on Sundays. This trend was started by Joseph Pulitzer (who later lent his name to the famous journalism awards) and the challenge was taken up by his chief rival, William Randolph Hearst (recognized as the model for the egocentric newspaper tycoon of Orson Welles's film *Citizen Kane*). The battle between these two giants of the popular press had profound implications for the comic strip.

ists in America. As well as Joe Keppler himself (and later his son, Udo Keppler) there were Thomas Sullivant, Eugene Zimmerman ('Zim'), Thomas Naste and many others. The first reprint compilation of **Puck** comic strips was published in 1899 by E.P. Dutton & Company of New York.

Judge (initially **The Judge**) was started on 29 October 1881 by James Wales, a talented former **Puck** cartoonist, who opposed that magazine's Democratic stance and turned **Judge** into a Republican rival (both publications remained overtly political). Although the newcomer

was not an immediate success, it had staying power and outlasted most of its rivals that were also jumping on the **Puck** bandwagon (**Chic, Tid-Bits, Rambler, Wasp** and so on). Like **Puck**, **Judge** attracted some of the finest American draftsmen. These included Norman Rockwell and Theodore Geisel (who later, as Dr Seuss, was to be the famed creator of many splendid children's books).

The third major cartoon magazine was **Life**, started by illustrator John Mitchell in January 1883. Both **Puck** and **Judge** made good use of colour but **Life**, in its early years, eschewed

Tycoons and founding fathers

Pulitzer's **New York World** was the first to have a Sunday supplement, and it included cartoons. Hearst went one better when he launched his own supplement to the Sunday **New York Journal**, the **American Humorist**, on 18 October 1896. As well as having cartoons, it also featured strips.

Pulitzer was well aware that strips helped to increase the number of papers sold. So was Hearst, but he also had a personal affinity for comics, an appreciation formed when

young. It gave him an edge in the use of this important circulation weapon. For many years the two newspaper barons vied to give their readers the best comic strips. The battle benefited both the comics and their creators. And pivotal among the latter were three men, variously regarded as the founding fathers of the comic strip: Richard Outcault, Frederick Opper and Rudolph Dirks.

Richard Felton Outcault (1863-1968) was primarily a **Life** and

Richard Outcault's bald big-eared urchin The Yellow Kid *at the opening of the Hogan's Alley Athletic Club*

Judge cartoonist but, as a prolific freelance illustrator, his work appeared in a number of different publications. Outcault created the first regularly appearing comic character to enjoy massive public popularity; that acclaim persuaded Pulitzer and Hearst that comics had an uplifting effect on circulations.

The feature that began it all was a cartoon about slums and back alleys where the (mainly) immigrant population lived.

After experiments with several titles, *Hogan's Alley* was finally

Richard Outcault's famous creation Buster Brown *is pictured here with his demonic dog Tige*

chosen as its regular heading. Readers, however, soon gave it a different name, *The Yellow Kid*, after its unsightly but endearing, night-shirted child star.

The *Kid* first appeared in two cartoon panels in Pulitzer's Sunday **New York World** on 5 May 1895. At first his nightshirt was blue; in fact, there was a marked absence of recognizable yellow in the paper's early attempts at colour as, for technical reasons, yellow was difficult to achieve. The challenge was taken up by the **World's** engravers who began to experiment. Needing a small area in the newspaper to work with, they chose the *Kid's* nightshirt. By 5 January 1896, they succeeded: it turned a bright, eye-catching yellow. From then on he became *The Yellow Kid*.

The *Kid* communicated with his public in a unique way. Instead of using word balloons, Outcault wrote funny messages on his shirt, which further endeared him to his many readers. The success of the feature (still called *Hogan's Alley* or variations of such) was not lost on William Randolph Hearst who lured Outcault away from his rival's newspaper to work for him on his own **New York Journal**.

Hearst asked Outcault to draw the *Kid* for his paper, gave it the official

title *The Yellow Kid*, and encouraged the artist to change it from a single panel to comic strip format. Joseph Pulitzer, predictably displeased, took legal action against Hearst. As a result, Pulitzer's **World** was allowed to retain rights to *Hogan's Alley* and its characters, and Outcault was similarly granted rights to continue the characters for the **Journal**. He did so for a couple of years before he tired of the *Kid* and returned to freelancing.

Perhaps the main reason why Outcault dropped the character was that he was unhappy with its vulgar reputation. Indeed, the *Kid* is credited with having introduced the term 'yellow journalism', as applied to the down-market press with its low news value and rampant sensationalism. But it did make him a great deal of money, thanks to the widespread merchandising. This included books of reprints: the first *The Yellow Kid* (1897) — more a joke magazine than a comic according to those who possess this rare item — and the second *The Yellow Kid at MacFadden's Flats*, a compilation of cartoons from the **Journal** linked by narrative text. *MacFadden's Flats*, in the opinion of some, constitutes the first true American comic book.

The *Kid* was not the only important character created by Outcault. On 4 May 1902 he started *Buster Brown* for the Sunday **New York Herald**. This was decidedly up-market; where *The Yellow Kid* had been a slum dweller, *Buster Brown* was the son of a well-to-do, upper class family. He had the look of an angel, the mind of a devil and actions to boot, with his dog Tige as a partner in crime. This strip, much more than *The Yellow Kid*, showed off to the full Outcault's considerable powers of draftsmanship: *Buster Brown* was not only hilarious to read but incredibly funny to look at as well. The feature's immense popularity led to a number of reprint volumes: the first, *Buster Brown and His Resolutions*, was published in 1903; it was followed in subsequent years by other volumes.

Frederick Burr Opper (1857-1937) had been for many years **Puck's** principal political cartoonist when he was spotted by Hearst's expert eye. He hired Opper in 1899 to draw cartoons for the **American Humorist**, the supplement to his **New York Journal**. That was where Opper's great comic character, a tramp called *Happy Hooligan*, first appeared on 26 March 1900.

Hooligan was popular with the public from the start and as Opper became more adept at the comic

HAPPY HOOLIGAN MAKES A CHRISTMAS CALL UPON SOME ENGLISH SWELLS

Happy Hooligan, the hugely popular hobo with the tin-can hat, was drawn by Frederick Opper for around thirty years

strip he began to introduce other characters who were equally successful, such as *Alphonse and Gaston* and a mule named *Maude*. The popularity of these strips was important because they very quickly inspired collections of reprints. Both *Alphonse* and *Gaston* and *Happy Hooligan* had strip compilations published in 1902.

These were long, thin hardback volumes 15¼ x 10 inches (39 x 25 cms), with half a Sunday comic's strip to a page, printed in full colour: this successful reprint formula became common in the early 1900s.

Incidentally, Opper for many years did not abandon his topical cartoons: Hearst allowed him space on an editorial page of his dailies to give full vent to his political expression.

Rudolph Dirks (1877-1968), another of the great founding fathers of the comic strip, was born in Germany and arrived in Chicago with his immigrant parents at the age of seven. An early contributor to **Life** and **Judge**, in 1897 he was invited to contribute to Hearst's **New York Journal**. Seeking a potential success like *The Yellow Kid*, Hearst asked Dirks to create something modelled

upon Wilhelm Busch's famous German strip, **Max und Moritz.**

Hearst was a long-time fan of Busch; from childhood he had delighted at the devilish tricks of **Max und Moritz** who were said to have kindled his interest in comic strips. Rudolph Dirks responded with exactly what was required. *The Katzenjammer Kids* made its début in the **American Humorist** supplement of the **Journal** on 12 December 1897.

The *Katzenjammer* cast of characters soon became familiar to millions of readers: *Mama, Hans and Fritz*, the *Captain* and the *(school) Inspector* all had German-English pidgin accents which endeared them to both the immigrant population and general public. After some fifteen years of creating *The Katzenjammer Kids* each week, Dirks moved to Pulitzer's **New York World**, taking his strip with him—not something Hearst would 'take lying down'! A court case resulted in a similar judgement to the one on *The Yellow Kid*; Dirks was allowed to keep the rights to the characters while Hearst retained the strip.

The artist who took over *The Katzenjammer Kids* in the **Journal** was Harold Knerr. Rudoph Dirks had to retitle the feature in the **World**: first *Hans and Fritz*, then *The Captain and the Kids*. Under the latter title it ran for years in parallel to the one drawn by Knerr. Both strips were excellent. Dirks's creative use of the comic strip medium paved the way for many imitators, while Knerr, also born into a German immigrant family, had a real understanding of the strip he had taken on – and enhanced it.

Again, from the very early years, collections of reprints in book form started to appear, adding to the growing number of published 'comic books'. The first of these was entitled simply *The Katzenjammer Kids*, published in 1902.

Newspaper comics were, in the main, reprinted by a handful of publishers. From 1901 Frederick A. Stokes & Company of East 16th Street, New York, issued books in the long oblong format of *Foxy Grandpaw*, a character created for Pulitzer's **New York Herald**. The same firm, from 1903, started to publish compilations of *Buster Brown* Sunday pages. And so it continued with various titles until about 1917 when Stokes reissued a number of their earlier volumes in cheap editions before ceasing publication of comic books (or possibly the firm went out of business).

Hearst's publishing company, **The New York American and Journal**, brought out some of its own reprint compilations with *Alphonse and Gaston*, *Happy Hooligan* and *The Katzenjammer Kids* being issued by the firm between 1902 and 1905. Later, however, Hearst seemed content to license the material to others, as too did Pulitzer with his published strips which were reprinted by firms such as Duffield & Company (New York) and Saalfield Publishing Company (Ohio).

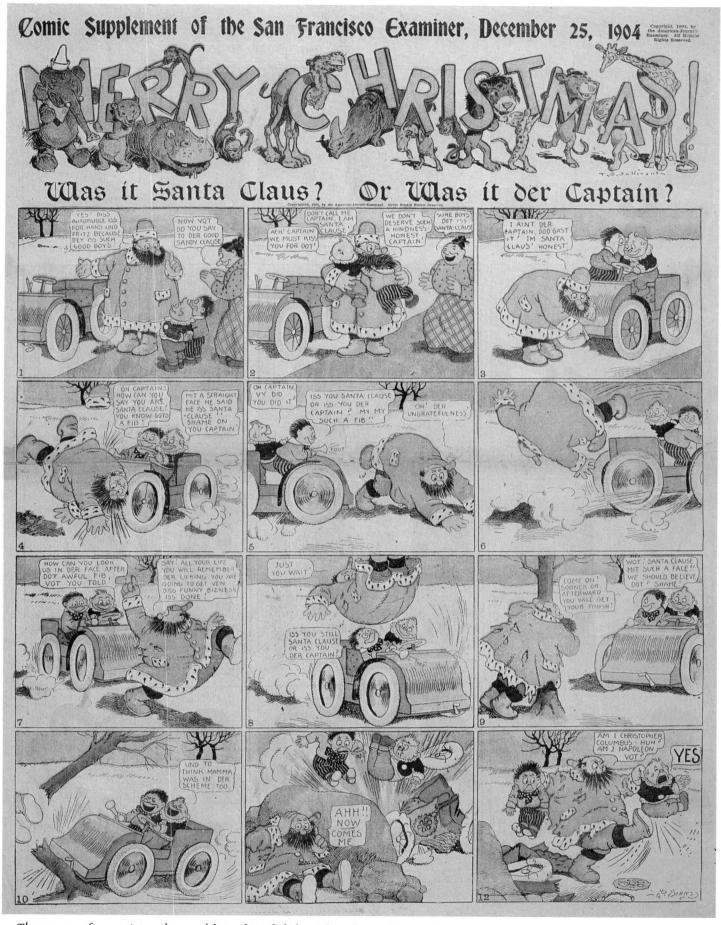

There were few artists who could rival Rudolph Dirks. Shown here is his greatest creation The Katzenjammer Kids, *modelled on the popular German characters,* Max und Moritz

Grand masters of US comics

The next three decades saw some of the world's greatest comic strips by the grand masters of the medium which are now acknowledged as classics of the genre. One of the greatest of them all was Winsor McCay, the creator of *Little Nemo in Slumberland*.

Winsor McCay (1867-1934) had very little tuition before becoming a leading comic artist in the early 1900s. He worked for a Dime Museum, drawing and painting promotional posters, before moving on to provincial newspapers and later accepting a position on the **New York Evening Telegram**, owned by James Gordon Bennett.

For the **Telegram** and another Bennett paper, the morning **Herald**, McCay drew various features which included several fantastic strips about dreams, the best remembered of these being *Dreams of a Rarebit Fiend*. This was humour based on the bizarre unsettling visions produced by the eating of Welsh Rarebit.

Similar McCay strips reflecting his fascination with dreams included *Dreams of a Lobster Fiend*, *Midsummer Dreams* and *Autumn Day Dreams*. Other fantastic features he drew were *Little Sammy Sneeze* (a boy with a hurricane-like sneeze) and *Hungry Henrietta* (a baby with a voracious appetite who aged visibly each week as the strip progressed). But McCay's greatest dream strip began on 15 October 1905. *Little Nemo in Slumberland* was a true classic that today inspires awe and reverence, being regarded as one of the greatest comic strips of all time.

Such an accolade is not due principally to its artistry. Although McCay was an excellent artist (as evidenced not only by his strips but also his many political and other cartoons), in *Nemo* his pen-work plays second-

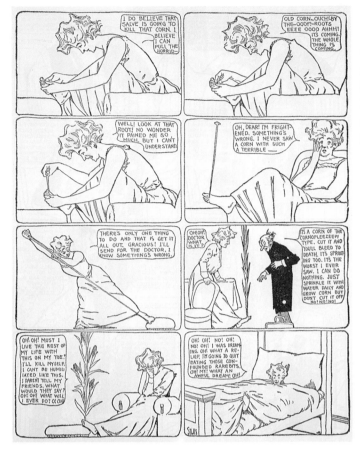

'Silas', the genius behind the bizarre Dreams of a Rarebit Fiend *was Winsor McCay: an example from 1905*

In the most celebrated comic strip of all time, Winsor McCay stunningly depicts the change from year 1908 to 1909. It appeared in **The New York Herald**, *27 December 1908*

fiddle to the fantastic vision, imagination, perspective and much more that flowed from his pen on to the page. Like D.W. Griffith and the movies, McCay did things with his medium that were daring, different and unprecedented – though widely emulated thereafter – setting the standard for much of comic art to come.

Winsor McCay was an artist with extraordinary talents. Those talents also extended to animation. His films *Gertie the Dinosaur* and *The Sinking of the Lusitania* pioneered the field.

The founders of the comic strip, Outcault, Opper and Dirks, together with that great master of the art form, Winsor McCay, were followed by a raft of others whose talents scaled new heights and who today are hailed as geniuses in their own right. Among them were Jimmy

Swinnerton, Bud Fisher, George McManus, Elzie Segar, George Herriman, Cliff Sterrett, Sydney Smith, Frank King, Harold Gray and Al Capp.

James ('Jimmy') Swinnerton (1875-1974) began his career on Hearst's **San Francisco Examiner** in 1892. Three years later he went to New York to draw for Hearst's **New York Journal**. Until he started *Jimmy*, as it was called originally, he had been known for his drawings of small bears and tigers which became big favourites with the readers of both papers. *Little Jimmy* did not become an additional daily newspaper comic strip until much later; 1904, after all, was early for the newspaper strip in the four-picture narrative form that we know today.

The first really successful six-days-a-week strip was *Mutt and Jeff* which began in 1907 and had an

incredibly long run – until 1982. Its creator was Harry Conway Fisher, known to all as 'Bud' Fisher, who earned so much money in those early years that by the Twenties and Thirties he was leaving most if not all of the work to assistants. Fisher's vast wealth stemmed from his foresight in copyrighting the strip in his own name and he was a millionaire for many years. He died in 1954.

Mutt and Jeff were a comedy team. *Mutt*, the tall one, was the schemer and *Jeff*, the short one, was his foil – although the latter often had the last laugh. The strip was not only popular in the US but also had international distribution.

George McManus (1884-1954) was an extremely talented draftsman whose work appeared both in the daily papers and Sunday supplements. After a succession of forgettable strips he scored a hit with *The Newlyweds* in the **New York World**. This resulted in an offer to work for William Randolph Hearst's **New York American** which he joined in 1912. A year later McManus created what was to become one of the most popular strips in American comics: *Bringing up Father*.

Known to millions as *Maggie and Jiggs*, it featured an Irish-American couple rocketed into the ranks of the *nouveau riche* with the first prize

from a lottery ticket. The theme of the strip for nigh on eighty years (for it is still running, drawn and written by others) was *Jiggs*'s unease with the new social class to which his wife *Maggie* aspired. He was more comfortable with the customers at Dinty's Saloon, preferring beer and corned beef and cabbage to wine and *French cuisine*. McManus's work was quite beautiful, with an Art-Deco look, particularly in the early years. His women – *Maggie* and her peers excepted – were gorgeous, with masses of hair curled into ringlets and their clothes looking as though they were straight off the page of the latest dress-designer's catalogue.

Popeye, Annie and Li'l Abner

Another legendary name in comics is that of Elzie Crisler Segar (1894-1938), the man who wielded the pen behind Popeye. The creator of the most famous seadog in comics was born in Illinois and began his career before he reached his teens, drawing cinema promotional material. After successfully completing a correspondence course in cartooning, Segar went to Chicago to work for the **Chicago Herald** in 1916.

After two or three forgettable Sunday funnies strips and following the buy-out of the **Herald** by Hearst, Segar moved to Hearst's **Chicago American** and then later to the **New York American** where *Thimble Theatre* made its début on 19 December 1919.

The feature was modelled on an existing strip, *Midget Movies* (later, *Minute Movies*) which parodied current silent box-office hits. *Thimble Theatre* was to have a similar theme but soon shifted its ground, as Segar found stories in his characters. And what characters! His most famous star, *Popeye*, took ten

years to arrive on the scene but when he did he stole the show. He became world-famous, as did his co-stars *Olive Oyl* and *J. Wellington Wimpy* (legend has it that his love of hamburgers inspired the owners of a British fast-food chain to name their restaurants after him).

E.C. Segar died of leukemia in 1938 but *Popeye* and *Thimble Theatre* were continued by others, notably Bud Sagendorf who took over daily and Sunday strips from 1958 but whose association with *Thimble Theatre* went back to the Thirties.

No discussion of newspaper comics would be complete without mention of George Herriman (1880-1944). Born in New Orleans, he moved with his family to Los Angeles and later was employed by the engraving department of a city newspaper. Ambitious to be a cartoonist, he went to New York and in the early 1900s his work appeared in **Judge** and **Life** as well as the **New York News** and the **New York American**.

Hearst liked his work and offered him a job in the art department of the **New York Journal**. It was there

that *Krazy Kat* was born, at first in guest appearances in another strip, then graduating to a daily (1913) and finally a full Sunday page (1916). *Krazy Kat* had a simple theme. The starring characters, a cat, dog and mouse trio, formed a bizarre love triangle: the cat was in love with the mouse, and the dog – *Police Officer Pup* – adored the cat.

Krazy, Officer Pup and *Ignatz Mouse* lived in Coconino County, a real place in name only. It was a weird desert setting with wild cacti in plant pots, changes in scenery like the swift movement of stage backdrops and a sky that changed colour from panel to panel as though viewed through a kaleidoscope.

Like Herriman, some artists became specifically identified with a strip other than with the broad range of their work. Cliff Sterrett (1883-1964) created one of the first comic strips with a female lead when *Positive*

George Herriman's classic Krazy Cat *with ever-changing scenery, strange dialogue and stranger relationships: 1936*

Polly (later changed to *Polly and her Pals*) started a forty-six year run on 4 December 1912. The focus of attention, however, quickly shifted to *Polly*'s father and it was from him and his interaction with others, particularly *Polly*'s friends, that Sterrett derived his humour.

Sydney Smith (1877-1935) was paid huge sums for *The Gumps*, a family saga that began in 1917. Smith died in a car accident in 1935 but, thanks to his having set up a team to ghost the strip for him, his creation continued for another twenty-five years, until 1959. Although *The Gumps* was drawn in Smith's somewhat basic style, it was nevertheless loved by millions as a comic soap opera. Smith's characters laughed, loved and even died throughout its long run.

Fame came also to a one-time assistant to Sydney Smith, Harold Gray (1894-1968), who created *Little Orphan Annie*. *Annie* first appeared on 5 August 1924 and from then until his death Gray worked on little else. *Annie* (still running, drawn by Leonard Starr) was distinctive for two things in particular. First, Gray

used the strip as a soapbox to sound off his strong opinions about life, social issues and politics; and second, the eyes of his characters were always left blank − two white ovals sitting in the centre of their countenances. Many liked the approach, saying it allowed the reader to interpret an expression freely. Others found it irritating, wishing the empty eye-sockets had been filled.

But Harold Gray's real ability was as a story-teller, and his strong opinions added spice. The veritable sermons with which he filled *Annie*'s word-balloons, often listened to in isolation by her dog *Sandy*, endured forty-four years.

Another first for newspaper comic strips occurred in *Gasoline Alley* which began in 1918. Initially the strip cashed in on the popular success of the motor car (hence the title) but it soon became a soap opera, notable for the ageing of its characters and small-town America story-lines.

The creator of *Gasoline Alley* was Frank King (1883-1969) who was

both artist and writer until the early Fifties and then, with assistance, until his death. By then it had been taken over almost entirely by Dick Moores (the daily) and Bill Perry (on Sundays). Other hands continue the work today, making it one of the oldest comic strips in existence.

Al Capp (1909-79) started his career like Harold Gray, for some years acting as assistant to an artist who already had a successful syndicated strip. Capp worked for Ham Fisher who initiated the popular boxing comic strip *Joe Palooka*, which ran from 1930 until 1984.

In 1934 Al Capp created the hugely popular *Li'l Abner*, a tale of hillbillies in the bucolic South that became one of the most successful comic strips of all time. Capp, too, had artistic assistants but still did the writing himself and was responsible for all the great story-lines and characters. Those characters were also given a big boost with the release of motion pictures in 1940 and 1957, the latter a musical, which added to Capp's fortune.

Space travel and detection classics

In 1926 science-fiction pioneer editor and publisher, Hugo Gernsback, launched the world's first science fiction (or SF) magazine, **Amazing Stories**, a bedsheet-sized pulp. The August 1928 issue featured *Armageddon 2419*, the exciting tale of *Anthony 'Buck' Rogers*, a man who slept for five hundred years before awakening in a war-torn America. In his introduction Gernsback trumpeted his pleasure, describing it as a 'real scientifiction story plus'. One

leading strip syndicate obviously agreed; they asked the writer, Philip Francis Nowlan, if he could adapt it into a comic strip.

Nowlan was quick to comply and the world's first science fiction daily strip appeared on 7 January 1929, followed a year later by a Sunday page. The artist was Dick Calkins (1895-1962) whose enthusiastic art threw at the public rocket-ships, war-machines, ray-guns and all manner of far-out gadgets. He worked on *Buck Rogers* with Nowlan until the writer died in 1940 and then Calkins became respon-

sible for both stories and art until 1947. After that a succession of artists and writers handled the strip until both daily and Sunday came to an end in the late Sixties.

Exactly five years later the rival King Features Syndicate responded with

A US Ex-Army pilot Dick Calkins was the artist for this episode of the classic science-fiction strip Buck Rogers in the 25th Century. Note the Thirties-style rocket ship, so beloved of Buck Rogers serials

Flash Gordon, which began with a Sunday page on 7 January 1934. The artwork was stunning — of a much finer quality than that of Calkins and Nowlan's 25th-century hero. It was superior to anything similar that had appeared in comics. Even today, nearly sixty years on, there are few penmen who can hold a candle to it. The artist responsible was Alex Raymond (1909-56).

Raymond drew in a style that was akin to fine art. Wonderful flowing lines, heavy atmospheric shading and classic figures, all contained in large roomy panels. Later he had the audacity to draw his Sunday page simply as two or three large pictures. But no one complained. The art was always too good.

Unlike *Buck Rogers*, *Flash Gordon* was set in the present day. It began with the planet Mongo hurtling towards the Earth while *Flash* and his voluptuous companion, Dale Arden, accompanied Dr Hans Zarkov in his rocket ship on a mission to the strange world. Thereafter followed exotic adventures on Mongo and battles with *Ming*, its merciless emperor.

The writer of *Flash Gordon* was Don Moore, who also scripted the daily strip (1940-44) that was drawn by Raymond's assistant, Austin Briggs. When Alex Raymond left the Sunday in 1944, Briggs took it over. Sadly, Raymond was never to return; he was killed in a car crash in 1956. Briggs was succeeded in about 1950 by Mac Raboy who drew it until his death in 1967. Since then it has been illustrated by Dan Barry.

Both *Buck Rogers* and *Flash Gordon* have inspired the movie moguls. First with several classic Thirties serials in which actor Buster Crabbe played *Buck* and *Flash*, and later a spoof movie (*Flesh Gordon: 1974*) and two TV series: *Buck Rogers in the 25th Century* (1950 and 1978).

It was also in the early Thirties that the first, and greatest, of the police-detective strips started. This was *Dick Tracy* by Chester Gould (1900-85), who originally conceived the character as *Plainclothes Tracy*. After a couple of trial Sunday pages, it began as a daily strip on 12 October 1931. It was in the middle of the Depression, at a time when Chicago's gangsters made the city synonymous with violent crime.

Not surprisingly, the Tracy strip focused on Chicago gangland. It struck the right nerve with readers who loved to see the mobsters getting what they deserved. Later in the Thirties when the Chicago gangs had been controlled, Chester Gould's stories shifted to the individual; and his characters, especially the villains, were nothing if not distinctive. The Blank wore a featureless mask; Flyface never bathed and, as a consequence, was always surrounded by flies; Haf-and-Haf had a face that was half ugly, half good-looking; Mole was a counterfeiter who lived in a sewer; among others were a wrinkly named Pruneface and a villain called Mumbles, the latter ordering up his crime in words which few people understood. Among the good guys were Tracy's girlfriend, Tess Trueheart and his adopted kid, Tracy Junior.

The most famous *Tracy* item created by Gould's fertile mind was the two-way wrist radio, a device that helped him communicate with his fellow officers. Later, it became a two-way television. At first it all seemed pure science fiction but inventions such as transistors and microchips have made Gould's creations a reality.

Chester Gould retired in 1977. Since then *Tracy* has been written by Max Collins. The artists have been former Gould assistants, Rick Fletcher (who died in 1983) and Dick Locher. The strip is still syndi-cated to hundreds of papers and in 1990 received revived attention due to a well-intentioned but rather lack-lustre movie starring Warren Beatty and Madonna.

Two other famous strips from the early Thirties — later christened the Golden Age of newspaper adventure strips — were *Mandrake the Magician* and *The Phantom*. Both were created by the same man, an ex-advertising agency copywriter named Lee Falk.

Falk had sold the idea for his first strip, about an archetypal stage magician, to King Features Syndicate. This started on 11 June 1934. *Mandrake* is a master of illusion — one hand gesture and his opponents see anything he wants them to see: a giant hand to carry them to jail, multiple versions of himself, smoke rings that encircle and hold them prisoner, and so on. Mandrake's close companions are Lothar, a huge black man who serves as friend and bodyguard, and his lady friend, a curvaceous brunette by the name of Narda.

The first artist was Phil Davis, who died in 1964 after thirty years on the strip. He was succeeded by Fred Frederick who still draws it today. Lee Falk has been the writer for an incredible fifty-seven years. The strip, both the daily and the Sunday, have been syndicated worldwide for most of that time.

Remarkably, Lee Falk is also the creator of another of the world's most popular comic strips, *The*

The Phantom, *the 'Ghost-Who-Walks, 'Man-Who-Can-Never-Die' here demonstrates how he earned his reputation*

The PHANTOM FACES BART'S EXECUTION SQUAD--SIX RIFLES FIRE -- THE PHANTOM FALLS--THE PHANTOM IS NAILED IN A BOX --

--AND THE BOX IS TOSSED INTO THE LAKE AND SINKS RAPIDLY.

UNDER WATER--AND SUDDENLY THE BOX IS OPENED ---

THE PHANTOM SWIMS A SHORT DISTANCE---

THEN REACHES THE SURFACE, HIDDEN BY REEDS.... *Tomorrow*- HOW COME ?

Phantom, which he started two years after *Mandrake*, on 17 February 1936. The story of *The Phantom* is one of the most stirring in comics. He is the last in a long line of justice-fighters; a tradition passed down from father to son for four centuries. *The Phantom* lives in the deepest jungle, his skull cave guarded by the dreaded Bandar pygmies. Superstitious natives believe him to be immortal and call him the 'Ghost-Who-Walks'.

In the strip's run of over half a century (which includes a Sunday page started in 1939) *The Phantom* has had three artists. After Ray Moore came Wilson McCoy, followed by Bill Lignante. Since 1963 the artist has been Sy Barry.

Lee Falk is still the writer at the age of eighty-six!

Reprints and originals

Much of the work of these great comic strip artists was collected together in book form. At first it was the Sunday funnies, reprinted in the oblong format mentioned earlier. Soon, it was the turn of the newspaper comic strip. By 1910 *Mutt and Jeff* had become popular enough to be merchandised and reprinted in books. These were hardcover, a single strip to a page (actual size) and therefore an unwieldy 5 x 15 inches (13 x 38 cms).

Sometimes newspaper strips were reprinted in the old format established by Frederick Stokes, E.P. Dutton and others when reprinting the Sunday pages of strips like *Buster Brown* or *The Katzenjammer Kids*, with two dailies per page. This tradition was continued by the Saalfield Publishing Company around 1917 in a slightly smaller size.

In 1919 the company had taken over publication of the *Mutt and Jeff* books and rearranged the four panels of each so that two of the pictures were placed above the other two. The result was a book measuring a square 10 x 10 inches (25 x 25 cms). Not surprisingly, being much easier to handle, it proved a success and led to the firm of Cupples and Leon reprinting other popular features in the same format throughout the Twenties. These included *The Gumps* and *Bringing up Father*.

The first comic book produced in the modern format: comprised of reprints, it was a promotion for the firm Proctor and Gamble

A rival, the Embee Distributing Company, began to issue similar square format comic books in 1922, pricing them at 10 cents (as opposed to Cupples and Leon's 25 cents) and issuing them some 25 times a year as **Comic Monthly**. These were, in fact, the first 10 cent monthly comic books.

Cupples and Leon, however, dominated the market until the early Thirties. Then Whitman Publishing of Racine, Wisconsin, launched its hugely popular *Big Little Book Series*. These were small, almost square, very thick books; they reprinted one comic panel on the right-hand page with the text on the left — the word-balloons having been removed.

The following year, in 1933, the Eastern Color Printing Company

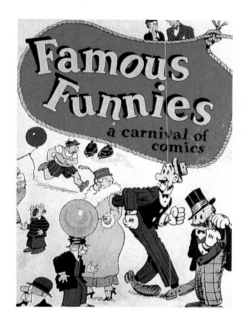

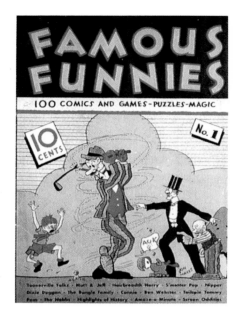

Three all-reprint **Famous Funnies**: *a promotional version, a ten-cent one for chain stores and No. 1 for the news-stands*

then presented it gratis with every purchase of a particular product. The comic was **Funnies on Parade** and was as close to the modern US comic book as it was possible to get. The contents were in full colour, there were several strips throughout, it was printed on standard paper (not stiff card) with a colour cover and it had thirty-two pages.

It inspired the Eastern salesman who created it, Max C. Gaines, not only to create other promotional giveaways but also to take the historic step forward of packaging such a product for news-stand distribution. The result was **Famous Funnies**, an all-colour comic book containing sixty-four pages of Sunday reprints priced at 10 cents. The date on the cover was July 1934.

The editor of **Famous Funnies** was Stephen Douglas who achieved a 200,000 issue circulation and some international distribution as well. It was certainly popular in Britain where, like other countries, the reprint material had not appeared before. It also inspired imitations (see **British Comics**: Gerald G. Swan). Soon there was new material too as Douglas started to commission some original pages.

The trend was inevitable; and in late 1935 **Famous Funnies** faced some competition. First there was **New Fun**, a tabloid-size comic dated February, which published entirely new material. Then, dated December 1935, came **New Comics**, the first comic book to have contents that were entirely original.

It was, said the editorial, 'the international picture story magazine' and cleverly drove home the advantages of reading **New Comics**

Major Wheeler-Nicholson's **New Comics** *was the first comic book with all original material*

instead of **Famous Funnies**, with phrases like 'never printed before anywhere' and 'we know your eyes won't suffer from strain while you enjoy these clearly drawn pictures and large readable text' (each page contained around half a dozen pictures as opposed to twenty or so in **Famous Funnies**).

Of course there were drawbacks: art and stories lacked the quality of the newspaper reprints and several pages were printed in black-and-white. But the benefits, which included sixteen extra pages, tended to outweigh such points and it soon became apparent that the news-stand comic book with original material was here to stay.

The man behind **New Comics** was Major Malcolm Wheeler-Nicholson (1890-1968), an ex-cavalry officer with a subsequently varied career. An itinerant traveller, who had made some money as a pulp writer, he was more of an ideas merchant than a businessman, losing control over his company, National Allied Publications, in 1937 just short of wealth and success. For that company soon became National Periodical Publications, later known as DC Comics.

Is it a bird? Is it a plane? No; it's the world's greatest
adventure strip hero making a big hit in the new
Action Comics. *The superhero had arrived*

Superman, Batman and Wonder Woman

The wealth and success that lay ahead stemmed from more than the originality of all the material within a comic book — although that was a good start. The main factor was the creation of the superhero. This started with the publication of **Action Comics** in June 1938.

The first issue pictured a man clad in a tight-fitting red, yellow and blue costume performing an impossible feat: single handedly lifting a car above his head, while its terrified occupants escaped and took to their heels. This heroic strongman was *Superman*, described in the opening page as the 'Champion of the Oppressed. The physical marvel who had sworn to devote his existence to helping those in need!' He proved to be all that and more.

Superman was the creation of two teenagers from Cleveland, Ohio: writer Jerry Siegel and artist Joe Shuster. From the viewpoint of a half-century later, it seems astonishing that the youngsters' creation was not accepted by the first publisher they approached, especially considering how popular comics were in the Thirties and how difficult it was to create something really different. Yet history records that it took the boys five years' effort before they found anyone who would give *Superman* a chance.

Siegel and Shuster had first thought of the character in about 1933. They were enthusiastic science fiction fans and the concept of *Superman* emerged from a variety of influences: pulp magazine and SF heroes, mythical gods and sheer wish-fulfilment of the ordinary male who, it appeared, had a secret longing to burst out of his meek, mild bespectacled exterior and become someone who could do almost anything. It has also been claimed that Philip Wylie's novel *Gladiator* (published in 1930) was an influence for it too featured a character possessed of extraordinary strength and powers.

For five years Siegel and Shuster attempted to sell *Superman* as a syndicated newspaper strip. When they finally succeeded in a sale to National for **Action Comics**, they cut up their strips and pasted them on to board to make up the comic-book page size.

No one guessed just how well *Superman* would do and the subsequent meteoric rise in circulation took everyone by surprise: evidently readers could not get enough of this exciting new character!

National responded quickly, giving **Superman** his own title in summer 1939, while still retaining his adventures in **Action Comics**. It also started the company thinking about other superheroes. Back in March 1937 Major Wheeler-Nicholson, following on from his earlier successes, had launched Number 1 of **Detective Comics**. Edited by Vincent Sullivan, it had since then featured a succession of detective crime fighters with the occasional page of joke cartoons for light relief. One of the incumbent artists was Bob Kane who was able to provide National with exactly what they were looking for, the perfect accompaniment to **Superman**, a colourful costumed character called *The Batman* for the May 1939 issue of **Detective Comics** (No. 27).

Batman (the 'The' was soon dropped) had no super-powers. Instead he relied on brains and athleticism to fight the criminal classes. And he boosted his chances with a rib-hugging garment modelled on that of a bat, using it to strike fear into the hearts of his adversaries.

Superman's secret identity was Clark Kent, a mild-mannered reporter on the *Daily Planet* newspaper. Shy of women, he was timid of danger. *Batman* was quite different. His alter-ego was Bruce Wayne, a rich playboy with girl-friends and a very different lifestyle. Soon **Batman** too was given his own title in spring 1940 — in addition to his adventures which continued to appear in **Detective Comics**.

The two heroes became the foundation of National's publishing empire. And shortly, as an acknowledgement, a soon-to-be-familiar symbol began appearing in the corner of all the firm's comics: a circle which contained the words, 'A Superman DC Publication' (the DC stood for **Detective Comics**). The characters, particularly *Superman*,

Detective Comics *No. 8: pre-super-hero crime stories; and No. 22: National's first masked hero,* The Crimson Avenger

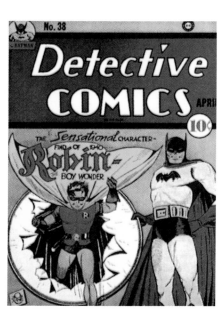

Detective Comics *No. 37: classic early* Batman *in his element; and No. 38: his sidekick* Robin 'The Boy Wonder' *is introduced*

A few months after he made his début in **Flash Comics** *(January 1940),* The Flash *appeared in* **All Flash Quarterly** *drawn by E.E. Hibbard (Summer 1941)*

Flash Comics *No. 26 (February 1942)*

All American Comics *No. 16, July 1940: first appearance of the original Golden Age* Green Lantern. *Art by Mart Nodell*

became a multi-million dollar industry with comic book sales, movie serials and extensive merchandising. But this was only the beginning for National.

What had been launched was a superhero boom. In rapid succession DC created other new heroes with super-powers: *The Flash* possessed super-speed, with a costume modelled on that of Mercury; *Green Lantern* had no powers but a ring which, thanks to its green ray, enabled him to do extraordinary things; *Wonder Woman*, a female version of *Superman*, had a magic lasso; *The Spectre*, a mystic character, was the spirit of a deceased policeman, *The Atom*, a pint-sized power-house, and *Hawkman*, a winged hero; and so on.

The 1940 winter issue of **All Star Comics** featured many of DC's heroes together, working as a team named *The Justice Society of America*. These adventures continued throughout the Forties and were hugely popular, although it was something of a challenge for writers to craft a smooth story around such a diverse group.

Of course, where there was big money to be made there was bound to be competition. Rivals to National issued several superhero-type comic books, following the success of *Superman*, with little lasting success. But the competition emerged in its most aggressive form starting with the publication of Marvel Comics in the autumn of 1939. The first issue is one of the most collected comics in existence, a mint copy fetching close to $100,000. The publisher was Timely Publications, owned by Martin Goodman. This was the forerunner of one of today's principal publishers of comics, Marvel Comics, the other, of course being DC Comics.

That first issue (with a cover by veteran science-fiction artist Frank

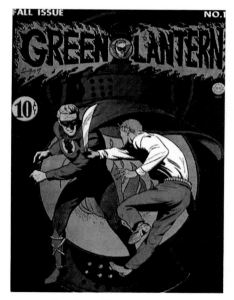

Soon after his **All American Comics** *début,* Green Lantern *was awarded his own title: Pictured here are No. 1 (Fall 1941) and No. 13 (Fall 1944)*

Wonder Woman *(Winter 1944): art by Harry G. Peter*

Wonder Woman *also starred in* **Sensation Comics***: issue April 1944 with art by Harry G. Peter*

The Justice Society of America *featured in fifty-seven issues of* **All Star Comics***. This issue is dated Dec-Jan 1942*

The Golden Age Sub-Mariner *and* Human Torch *battle it out in this July 1940 issue of* **Marvel Mystery Comics***. Art by Bill Everett*

The origin of the ghostly hero The Spectre *appeared in this issue of* **More Fun Comics**

An early Fifties crime comic (October 1952)

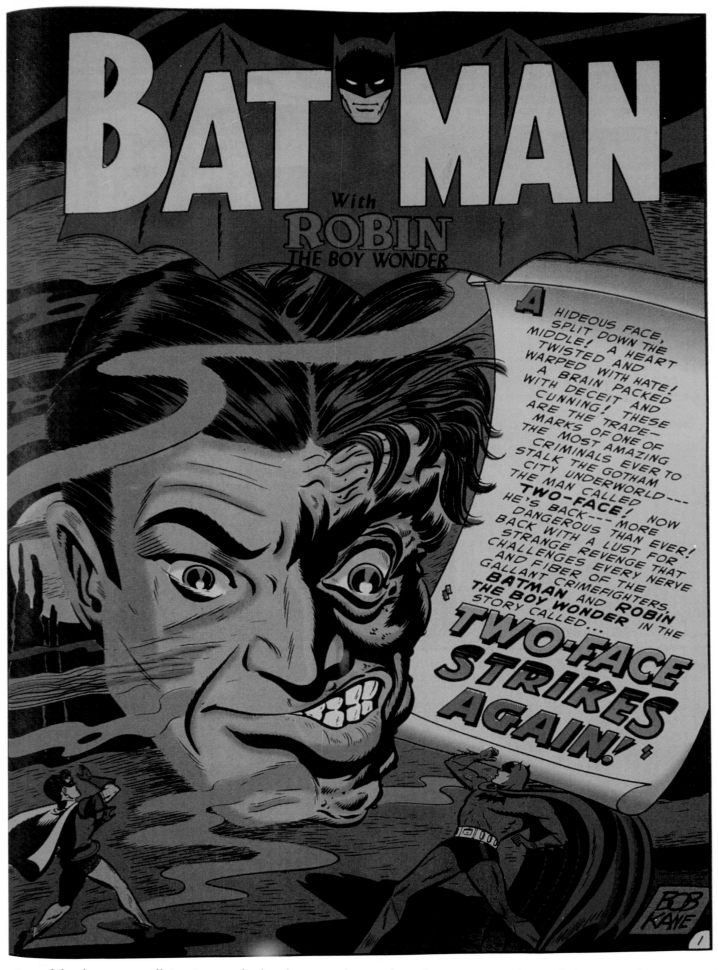

One of the dangerous villains Batman had to face was the psychopathic Two-Face who made his crime decisions on the toss of a coin. Art was by Dick Spang and Charles Paris and not Bob Kane. **Batman** No. 81: February 1954

R. Paul) featured two of Marvel's greatest future heroes: *The Human Torch* and *Sub-Mariner*. The Torch differed from his peers across the rest of the industry by not being human. He was an android, created in a laboratory. *Sub-Mariner* was the half-human denizen of an undersea kingdom (later identified as Atlantis) and, at first, was portrayed as a villain seeking revenge on the surface humans for wrongs committed against his race. But soon all that changed. The big news was the war in Europe and there were real enemies to fight.

A wave of patriotism broke over the comic book publishing industry, symbolized perfectly by *Captain America*, the creation of writer-and-artist team Joe Simon and Jack Kirby. He wore a tight-fitting uniform modelled on the flag, swashbuckler's boots and gloves, and carried a shield. *Captain America* was the archetypal national patriot, taking the war to Hitler's chin with a firmly planted fist! When Simon and Kirby moved on a year or so later, their places were taken by a number of writers and artists, notably Bill Finger (who also scripted *Batman*) and Alex Schomburg (who became a respected science-fiction artist).

Timely Comics produced some of the best comic covers of the war. *The Human Torch, Sub-Mariner* and *Captain America* appeared in issue after issue, fighting the Germans and trouncing the Japanese. Not to be outdone, National's *Superman* walked arm-in-arm with members of the forces, tackled German patrol boats with bare knuckles and rode bombs down to their targets. Meanwhile *Batman* and his young side-kick, *Robin*, kept the American Eagle flying with his exhortations to buy war bonds and stamps.

Batman also acquired an innovative line-up of villains inspired, in part, by the weird characters encoun-

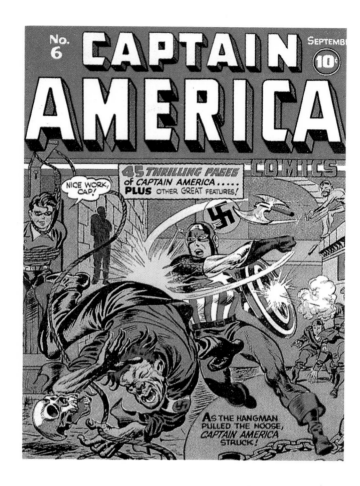

Captain America deals with the Nazi threat (September 1941). Art by Jack Kirby

One of the many excellent covers produced in the early Forties by Jerry Robinson and Bob Kane (April–May 1942)

tered by *Dick Tracy*. The best was *The Joker*, a lethal opponent who, in appearance, was a cross between the image on a playing card and cinema's Conrad Veidt in *The Man Who Laughs*. Almost as good was *Two Face*, a schizo-homicidal lunatic who decided whether or not to commit his crimes on the toss of a partly defaced coin. Another, *The Penguin*, was a deadly, umbrella-toting, rotund little man who wore a monocle and evening dress to mimic his namesake's appearance.

In 1940 *Batman* acquired a young partner, *Robin* (his creator claimed his name and outfit were based more on Robin Hood than a bird), and, in no time at all, it seemed as if all the superheroes were following suit. *The Human Torch* was accompanied by *Toro*, *Captain America* by *Bucky*, and so on. Young readers were supposed to identify with these junior versions of their heroes and their involvement meant to give an added boost to circulation.

But did it work that way? Not if you were Jules Feiffer, the famous cartoonist and comics aficionado, who gave his thoughts on the subject in his excellent book **The Great Comic Book Heroes**. Feiffer seemed to speak for many when he said: 'I couldn't stand boy companions. If the theory behind [them] was to give young readers a character with whom to identify it failed dismally in my case. The *grownups* were the ones I identified with. They were versions of me in the future. There was still time to prepare.' A little later Feiffer added: 'You can imagine how pleased I was when, years later, I heard [Robin] was a fag.'

This was a reference to some simple-minded logic in **Seduction of the Innocent** (1953), a book by Dr Frederick Wertham which claimed that Batman and Robin's life together had homosexual undertones. Wertham conducted a personal vendetta against comics in

A minor hero with a long life, Blue Beetle *was drawn by Charles Nicholas (pen-name for Charles Wojtkowski) in this July–August issue of 1940*

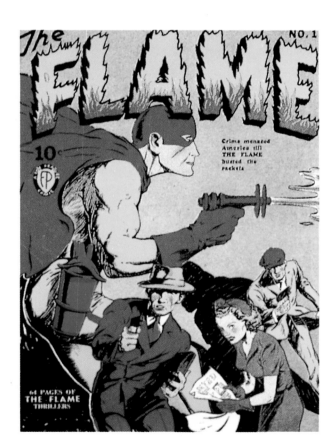

Artist Lou Fine contributed to this short-lived superhero title (Summer 1940)

Nicknamed 'The Big Red Cheese', the World's Mightiest Mortal in his own magazine (October 1941) and in **Whiz Comics** *(June 1943)*

the late Forties and early Fifties — which will be examined shortly.

The superhero boom of the early Forties also created a plethora of uniformed crime fighters in titles not published by either National or Timely. These are now largely forgotten but, for the record, included *Wonder Man, The Flame, The Green Mask, The Blue Beetle* (all Fox Publications), *The Masked Marvel* and *Amazing Man* (Centaur Publications). These enjoyed mixed success but most did not survive for very long.

Nearly all of the Golden Age superheroes were men. The main exception was *Wonder Woman*, an Amazon princess with superstrength, a magic lasso and bracelets that deflected bullets fired at her. She travelled in an invisible robot plane, drawn as though it were made of glass. She, too, had a secret identity: Diana Prince. She also had the male equivalent of *Superman*'s girlfriend Lois Lane, an army officer named Steve Trevor. *Wonder Woman* was the creation of

William Moulton Marston — a psychologist who wrote under the pseudonym Charles Moulton. In the early days her adventures were drawn by Harry G. Peter.

Rival publisher Fawcett came up with one of the most powerful of *Superman*'s rivals: *Captain Marvel,* 'the World's Mightiest Mortal'. *Superman* had to hide in alleys or dash into telephone booths to change from Clark Kent into his alter-ego. The Captain's transformation was more dramatic. He simply said the word 'Shazam' and, with a bolt of lightning and a clap of thunder, he changed from kid reporter Billy Batson into a crimson-clad giant of a man with the powers of Solomon, Hercules, Atlas, Zeus, Achilles and Mercury.

Christened 'The Big Red Cheese' by his arch-enemy Dr Sivana, *Captain Marvel* was the creation of writer Bill Parker and artist Charles Clarence (C.C.) Beck. It was perhaps too big a hit on the Forties comic scene: National hit Fawcett with a lawsuit alleging that similarities between

Captain Marvel and *Superman* were too great. Eventually, Fawcett gave in and the Captain disappeared. Years later things came full circle when DC bought the rights and revived the character.

The Big Red Cheese was popular overseas too. In Britain his adventures were reprinted by L. Miller & Son. When the supply of *Captain Marvel*'s adventures dried up, as a result of the legal dispute between National and Fawcett, Miller, with the Mick Anglo Studios, started his own hero title — **Marvelman** — together with two companion weeklies, **Young Marvelman** and **Marvelman Family**. The Anglicized version of *Captain Marvel* had newspaper copyboy Micky Moran changing into *Marvelman* by speaking the word 'Kimota' (to be read backwards for its concession to the atomic age). This, and the spin-offs, ran for years and the character has recently been revamped for US distribution under the title **Miracleman**. It remains an interesting example of cross-fertilization on the international scene.

Action Comics
No. 108 (May 1947)

Adventure Comics
No. 156 (September 1950)

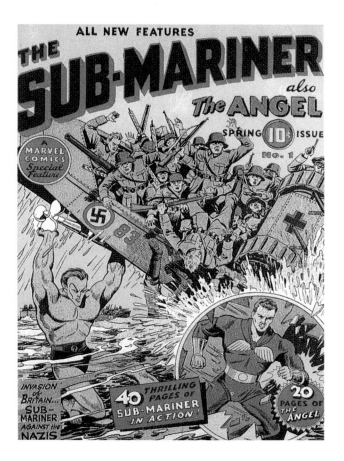

World's Finest Comics
No. 23 (July–August) 1946

The Sub-Mariner
No. 1 (Spring 1941)

Romance, crime and horror

Comic books and superheroes boomed throughout the war but after 1945 the genre entered a decline that would last for more than a decade. Patriotic stars like *Captain America* lost their glister and even the big draws such as *The Human Torch, Sub-Mariner, Green Lantern* and *The Flash* gradually winked out of existence.

More fortunate were the really big stars: *Superman, Batman* and *Wonder Woman*. The first two were popular enough to sustain appearances in more than one magazine: *Superman* in **Action Comics, Superman** and **Adventure Comics**; *Batman* in **Detective Comics** and **Batman**. Both appeared together, too, in **World's Finest Comics**. And the *Superman* character was strong enough to provide a new title in 1949: **Superboy**, described as 'The Adventures of Superman when he was a boy'.

Between 1945 and the late 1950s various attempts were made to rejuvenate the comic book industry and get it moving again. One of the first attempts was made by the ace writer and artist team of Joe Simon and Jack Kirby, who had created *Captain America* for Timely and winners like *Boy Commandos* for DC.

It was Simon who came up with the idea for a new title called **Young Romance** with stories about teenage girls in various love scenarios. He immediately went to his longtime partner Jack Kirby to draw it. The strong scripts and powerful art made **Young Romance** Number 1 (September/October 1947) a sellout and soon they created an equally successful sister publication called **Young Love**. Scores of similar titles from other publishers followed. Almost overnight Simon and Kirby found they had created a new genre, one that was to be amazingly successful through the Fifties and Sixties.

Young Romance No. 3 (January–February 1948): one of the first romance comics. Art by Jack Kirby

The adventures of Superman *when he was a boy had appeared since 1946 in* **Adventure Comics**. *In 1949* Superboy *was awarded his own title. Art by Wayne Boring*

Typical shock-value covers from the EC stable. **Tales from the Crypt** *No. 41 (May 1954).*
Art by Jack Davis. **Vault of Horror** *No. 30 (April—May 1953). Art by Johnny Craig*

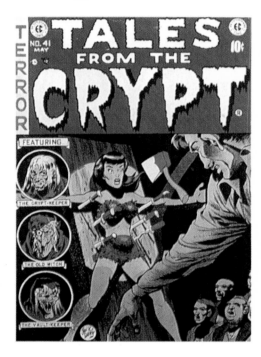 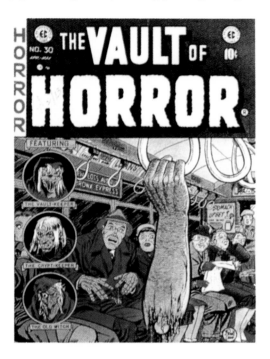

EC science fiction in **Weird**
Science *No. 5 (January—February*
1951). Art by Al Feldstein

The romance comics had their critics. According to Joe Simon in his fine book, **The Comic Book Makers**, Martin Goodman said the stories in **Young Romance** 'bordered on pornography'. Although this was wide of the mark — and Goodman himself was soon turning out similar titles — it was nothing to what was said about the next genre to be exploited: horror. Horror came in no-holds-barred strong scripts and powerful art that was designed to shock. It became the hallmark of its publisher: EC Comics.

EC originally stood for Educational Comics, a firm founded by Maxwell Charles Gaines just after the war; they published improving titles such as **Picture Stories from the Bible** and **Picture Stories from American History**. When Gaines died in 1947, his son William M. Gaines inherited the company and in 1950 changed its name to Entertaining Comics.

After a brief flirtation with crime and romance titles like **War Against**

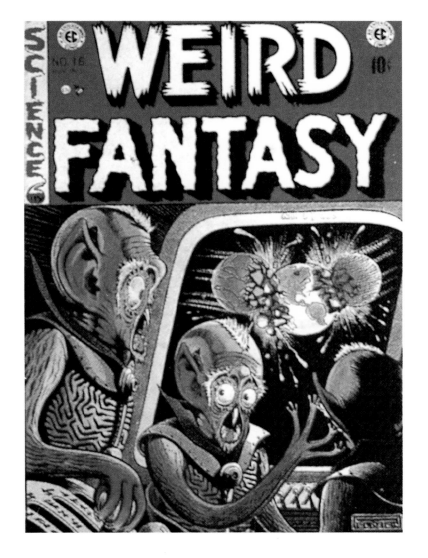

EC's Weird Fantasy *No. 16 (November–December 1950) Art by Al Feldstein*

Crime, Crime Patrol, Moon Girl and **Saddle Romances,** during 1947-50, Gaines decided to offer another kind of entertainment completely. These publications were transformed into **Vault of Horror** (April-May 1950), **Crypt of Terror** (April-May 1950) which became **Tales from the Crypt,** **Weird Fantasy** (May-June 1950), and **Weird Science** (May-June 1950). He later added two more titles: **Frontline Combat** (July-August 1951) and **Shock Suspenstories** (February-March 1952).

The horror comics featured strong stuff: rotting corpses, decapitation, children who killed their parents, hanging, shooting, stabbing, poisoning – in fact, murder of every description and depicted in the most graphic terms the artist could show. This was particularly effective as the draftsmen involved were some of the best in the business – among them Reed Crandall, Johnny Craig and Jack Davis.

EC's science-fiction titles, **Weird Fantasy** and **Weird Science,** were

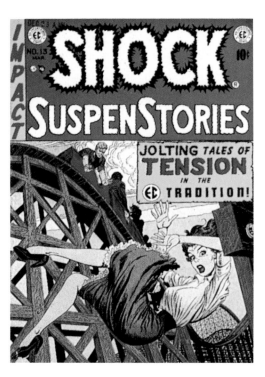

EC's Shock SuspenStories *No. 13 (March 1954) Art by J. Kamen*

73

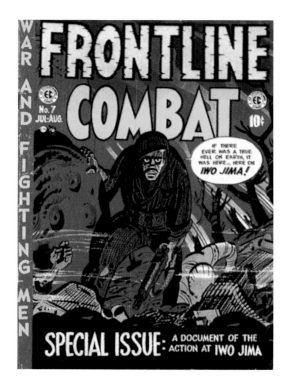

Realistic war stories from EC in
Frontline Combat
*No. 7 (July–August 1952).
Art by Harvey Kurtzman*

EC's **Two-Fisted Tales**
*No. 18 (November–December 1950).
Art by Harvey Kurtzman*

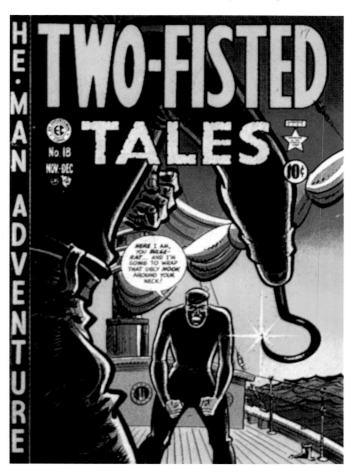

frequently drawn by the likes of Joe Orlando, Wally Wood, Al Williamson, Roy Krenkle and Frank Frazetta, all extraordinarily talented artists. Not as gruesome as their horror counterparts, the SF titles had some classy scripts, which sometimes were adaptations of stories by Ray Bradbury and H.P. Lovecraft. Other contributors included Harry Harrison, the noted science fiction writer, and Harvey Kurtzman.

Kurtzman was an artist as well as a writer. His artwork appeared in **Frontline Combat** and **Two-Fisted Tales**, two impressive war comics which he also edited for William Gaines and which refused to glorify combat and killing. The accent was on realism, and so impressive were they that the two titles are still highly sought after and reprinted today, some forty years on.

As superheroes began to wane and other genres replaced them in popularity, the comic book industry came under the scrutiny of a well-known psychiatrist, Dr Frederick Wertham. His attention was particularly caught by the crime and horror titles. Crime comics, he felt, frequently showed sex and violence to an unnecessary degree, despite their overall message (typical titles: **Crime Does Not Pay; Gangsters Can't Win**, and so on); whereas horror comics seemed to have no socially redeeming features at all.

In the early Fifties Wertham contributed articles to magazines which detailed his thoughts on the effects of comic books on the nation's youth. In 1954 he published what is now a famous book, **Seduction of the Innocent**, which drove home hard his conclusions that comics were a corrupt influence. EC comics, in particular, came in for a real roasting. When people across the country had their attention drawn to these, they accepted that Wertham might have a valid point.

The result was the establishment of the Comics Code Authority (CCA), a self-regulatory body established by the publishers to set standards and ensure that they would be upheld. Just two of the requirements were enough to put EC out of business overnight: 'All scenes of horror, excessive bloodshed, gory or gruesome crimes, depravity, lust, sadism, masochism shall not be permitted'; and, so that there was no doubt as to whom the code was aimed, 'No comics magazine shall use the word horror or terror in its title.'

Thereafter, parents made sure that their children read only comics with the CCA stamp in the corner of the front cover. Many newsagents simply would not accept any other and leading distributors were not prepared to carry them. Only the most obviously innocuous titles were able to escape CCA branding and survive. William Gaines was forced to abandon his entire EC line with but one exception: **Mad**, a new comic created and edited by Harvey Kurtzman.

Mad started in the autumn of 1952. Completely uninhibited, it specialized in wacky — some said 'college' — humour and send-ups of the media, including comic books, movies, television programmes and advertising. The humour was Kurtzman's and an almost immediate success. In 1955 Gaines turned it from a 10 cent comic book into a 25 cent magazine to avoid it being caught in the effects of the controversy then raging over the industry. It worked and, over the years, **Mad**'s circulation climbed impressively. Kurtzman left the magazine shortly afterwards but he was replaced by a series of editors who have since been responsible for its continued success. The famous **Mad** mascot, Alfred E. Neuman, has been a regular feature since 1955.

Dizzying cover art perspective from the pen of Charles Biro for the archetypal crime comic **Crime Does Not Pay** *(July 1944)*

Mad, *when it was an EC comic. No. 9 (March 1954). Art by Harvey Kurtzman*

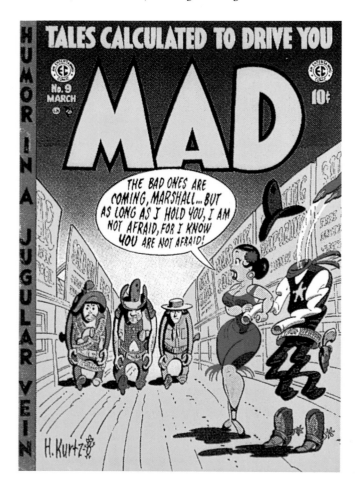

*Little Lulu No. 45 (March 1952).
Art by John Stanley*

**Walt Disney's Comics and
Stories** *No. 6 (March 1941)*

Dell and Disney

One publisher never to have any trouble with Frederick Wertham was Dell, which issued **Walt Disney's Comics and Stories, Little Lulu** et al. The company's name was taken from the first syllable of that of its originating owner, George T. Dellacorte, an industry pioneer. Way back in 1929 Dellacorte had published the tabloid-size **The Funnies**. It looked like a Sunday newspaper section and was notable for the fact that the strips it featured were original and not reprints.

The Funnies did not succeed (possibly because people were unwilling to pay for something that looked as though it should be free with their weekly newspaper) but Dellacorte went on to publish several other titles in the Thirties. Many of them were packaged by M.C. Gaines, following his success with **Funnies on Parade**, and **Famous Funnies**. Dell's Thirties' titles included **Popular Comics** (February 1936), **The Funnies** (October 1936) and **The Comics** (March 1937).

A big breakthrough came for Dell in 1940 when the firm came to an arrangement with Walt Disney Studios to produce a new title based on Disney's characters. Issued in October of that year, it was entitled **Walt Disney's Comics and Stories (WDCAS)**. It would last for years, its early success leading Dell to negotiate for the rights to other animated cartoon and movie characters, among them *Bugs Bunny, Little Lulu, Mickey Mouse, Woody Woodpecker, Popeye, The Lone Ranger, Roy Rogers* and *Tarzan*.

Dell was both lucky and skilful in its employment of creators — the men and women who wrote and drew the stories that appeared. First and foremost was Carl Barks who, from 1942 until the mid-1960s, was the anonymous artist (the only signature that could appear was that of Walt Disney) behind the duck tales that appeared in **WDCAS**. Barks wrote the stories too and created several new characters: Uncle Scrooge, a miser who kept his immense wealth in money bins, Gladstone Gander, the luckiest bird in creation, and Gyro Gearloose, a duck inventor. Carl Barks wove them all into witty and intelligent stories.

Disney was no less fortunate in having Floyd Gottfredson depict his flagship character, *Mickey Mouse,* in Dell comics. Actually, by the time he arrived at Dell, Gottfredson was an old hand at the Disney mouse. He had been responsible for the daily *Mickey Mouse* newspaper strip since 1930 and continued to draw it until 1975. Like Barks, Gottfredson was both a splendid writer and an excellent artist.

Little Lulu had been started in 1935 by Margorie Henderson Buell (Marge) in the **Saturday Evening Post**. There, it was a silent gag panel that had replaced its predecessor *Henry* by Carl Anderson. *Lulu*'s popularity was such that she starred in several animated films and via that route came to the attention of Dell. Her first appearance within Dell publications was in 1945 and the man who wrote and drew her adventures — anonymously — was John Stanley. Again, clever and witty scripts were blended with a pleasant drawing style to produce some memorable comics. Like Barks, Stanley also took the opportunity to create some new characters, all in keeping with *Lulu*'s world, which was essentially the neighbourhood as seen through children's eyes.

By the early Sixties Dell had a huge publishing empire, its comics selling in the hundreds of millions per year. But where formerly the animated or movie stars were an instant boost to profits, with hefty increases in licensing fees, they soon became a drain. A price rise on all titles to 15 cents turned out not to be the answer when other publishers could undercut them at 3 cents less. As a result, Dell surrendered its best titles to its partner, Western Printing and Lithography, who began issuing many of the same comics in a new line called **Gold Key Comics**. Dell started new titles featuring in-house characters but never again achieved the publishing heights it had reached in the Forties and Fifties.

Baby Huey
*No. 8
(November
1957)*

End of an Era

Another long-running comics publisher was Harvey Comics, started in 1939 by two brothers, Leon and Alfred Harvey. Initially the company published adventure and superhero titles such as **The Green Hornet**, adapted from the popular radio show. After the war, however, Harvey began to produce titles based on Sunday newspaper comic supplement strips. These included **Joe Palooka** (November 1945), **Terry and the Pirates** (April 1947), **Dick Tracy** (March 1950) and — highly popular — **Blondie** (March 1950) and **Dagwood** (September 1950).

Looking for areas to expand, Harvey took a leaf from Dell's book and negotiated with a film company — in this case Paramount — for the rights to use its line of animated cartoon characters. Thus Harvey was soon able to launch what were to be three of its most popular titles: **Casper the Friendly Ghost, Little Audrey** and **Baby Huey**. The firm had noticed a

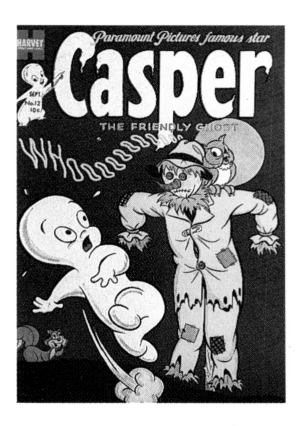

Casper the Friendly Ghost *No. 12*
(September 1953)

Little Audrey *No. 5 (August 1949)*

gap in the market – for a very young readership of seven or less – which at the time was not being catered for by its rivals.

So Casper, Audrey and Baby Huey were supplemented with titles such as **Little Dot** (September 1953), **Little Lotta** (November 1955), **Spooky the Tuff Little Ghost** (November 1955), **Hot Stuff the Little Devil** (October 1957), **Wendy the Good Little Witch** (August 1960) and **Ritchie Rich** (November 1960). All of them were used extensively in various Harvey titles, two of the most popular being *Casper* and *Ritchie Rich* spin-offs. Throughout the Fifties and Sixties these titles made a considerable impact. They

were always entertaining and well-written and certainly continued to be read by many youngsters who by rights should have outgrown them.

Whilst Harvey focused on a very young readership, another publisher became highly successful targeting the teenage market. This was Archie Comic Publications which started in 1939 as MLJ Magazines. Like other companies at the time, its first comic book offerings featured superheroes such as *Black Hood*, *The Hangman* and *The Shield*. However, in 1941 a red-haired, freckled teenager who wore bow-ties, lettered sweaters and checked trousers was introduced in the December issue of **Pep Comics**.

His name was *Archie Andrews* and his world was the epitome of small-town middle-class America. *Archie* and his pal *Jughead* (a wise-cracking hamburger-eating misogynist wearing a crown-shaped hat) attended Riverdale High with the strip's other stars, blonde Betty Cooper and rich brunette Veronica Lodge: a constant theme was the two girls' battle for Archie's attentions.

Archie Andrews was the creation of artist Bob Montana, although as he became more and more popular other hands were recruited. He became the star of **Pep Comics**, was given his own title, **Archie Comics**, in 1942, and went on to become the lead feature in **Laugh Comics**. By the late Forties two companion titles had been launched: **Archie's Pal**

Little Dot *No. 17 (May 1956)*

Archie *No. 24 (January 1947)*

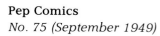

Pep Comics
No. 75 (September 1949)

Jughead and **Archie's Girls Betty and Veronica.**

Since then *Archie*'s popularity seems to have faded not a jot. Apart from the comics, he has been the star of an animated television show and a radio show, and has been extensively merchandised. To date, there have been countless spin-off titles. *Archie* looks set to continue into the next century.

The last of the really big comic book publishers to make its mark post-war was Charlton Comics, whose first comic book was issued in March 1946. However, very few titles followed until the mid-Fifties when the company took advantage of the Comics Code Authority stamp to issue dozens of 'clean' science fiction, western and romance books. As a result, business boomed.

Although none of the titles was memorable, Charlton was able to attract the talents of some top artists including, notably, Steve Ditko and John Severin. The fact that the titles lacked the appeal of those issued by some other publishers may have been due, in part, to the printing processes used. For some reason the colour on Charlton's comic book pages appeared greyer and flatter than their rivals. The company stayed in the comic book business until the mid-Eighties, when it sold off its characters to DC Comics.

By the end of the Forties the Golden Age of comics was over. The comic book industry had fallen into the doldrums. Superheroes were out of favour and the other genres also had their problems. The popularity of television worsened the situation, and the overall picture – Dell and Harvey being notable exceptions – was one of declining sales. Fortunately, thanks to a small group of individuals, led by Julius Schwartz, Mort Weisinger and Stan Lee, the Silver Age was about to dawn.

Classic Fifties science fiction in the three great DC titles shown on this page

My Greatest Adventure
No. 8 (March–April 1956)

Strange Adventures
No. 22 (July 1952)

Tales of the Unexpected
No. 14 (June 1957)

More DC science fiction in
Mystery in Space *No. 5*
(December–January 1952)

DC, Marvel and the Silver Age

Schwartz was an editor at DC Comics who had been on the lookout for new ideas throughout the early Fifties, having been responsible for introducing a line of science fiction and horror comics that sold well and had no trouble complying with the Comics Code. They were **Strange Adventures** (August 1950), **Mystery in Space** (April 1951), **House of Mystery** (December 1951), **My Greatest Adventure** (January 1955), **Tales of the Unexpected** (February 1956) and **House of Secrets** (November 1956). It was in March 1956 that DC Comics, with Schwartz as editor, launched **Showcase**, a title that would allow new ideas and heroes a trial run.

Schwartz's brainwave was to feature in **Showcase** Number 4, a rejuvenated version of one of DC's most popular Golden Age heroes, *The Flash*. Out went the winged hat, blue tights, winged boots and other paraphernalia of the original; in came a sophisticated streamlined version dressed in a skin-tight scarlet suit who was faster and had greater powers than his Forties counterpart. Three more **Showcase** appearances convinced DC that sales would support a regular title and thus was launched **The Flash** Number 105 (numbering continued from the old series) dated February 1959.

The Flash was immediately exciting. It was intelligently written by John Broome and stylishly drawn by Carmine Infantino, an artist who seemed to have been in waiting for the moment all his life. Infantino's depiction of speed was particularly well executed; few have ever done it

DC bring back their Golden Age hero **The Flash**. *It was the dawn of the Silver Age.*
Showcase *No. 14 (June 1956)*

First issue of **Justice League of America** *(October–November 1960) the Silver Age equivalent of the* **Justice Society**

better. Moreover, *The Flash* was given several appropriate super-villains to pit himself against. All of them, despite being fantastic, were ultimately believable.

Revamping *The Flash* paved the way in the next few years for other Forties superheroes to take their costumes out of mothballs and emerge from retirement. **Showcase** and a companion, **The Brave and the Bold,** were the launchpad for several new titles in the the late Fifties and early Sixties. Among them were **Green Lantern, The Atom, Hawkman** and **Justice League of America,** all revamps of Golden Age characters. It was the start of a revivalist boom that would continue throughout the Sixties.

Mort Weisinger was another important editor at DC, who had been with the firm since the early Forties. In the Fifties he was kept busy as story-editor on the *Superman* television show, in addition to his editorial duties, but when the show stopped in 1957 Weisinger began to look for other ways to stimulate the circulation of comic books featuring *Superman*.

Superman was then starring, remarkably, in seven different titles: **Superman, Action Comics, World's Finest** (with *Batman*), Adventure

First appearance of Braniac, arch-villain of the spaceways in **Action Comics** *No. 242 (July 1958)*

Following four appearances in **Showcase,** *The Flash was given his own title, which started from No. 105 (February–March 1959). The numbering followed on from where the Forties' title had stopped.*

Superman *No. 128 (April 1959)*

perman's Pal Jimmy Olsen
No. 12 (April 1956)

Detective Comics
No. 229 (April 1956)

Comics and Superboy as well as Superman's Girl Friend Lois Lane and Superman's Pal Jimmy Olsen. Justice League of America would soon make it eight.

Weisinger had showed innovation already in launching the Jimmy Olsen title in 1954 and Lois Lane (as a result of success in Showcase) in 1958. But he was aware, especially as so many featured the same characters, that the stories needed a boost as well, too many of them being dull, boring and repetitive. He recruited Otto Binder, a prolific writer responsible for many of the *Captain Marvel* scripts back in the Forties, and asked him to supply stories for his lead titles. Weisinger and Binder contributed in equal proportions many of the ideas that have today become an established part of the *Superman* legend.

Between them, in the space of a few short years, the two men created the Phantom Zone (a place where *Krypton* had imprisoned his criminals), *Bizarro* (an imperfect version of *Superman* who did everything backwards), *Supergirl* (*Superman*'s teenage cousin), the Fortress of Solitude, the Kryptonian city of Kandor (reduced and placed in a bottle by space villain *Brainiac*) and varieties of Kryptonite other than green — to name but a few of the additions. As a result of this, *Superman* became more than just a one-dimensional character; he turned into an individual and a human being. Other writers were part of this process, too, notably the co-creator Jerry Seigel who had been away from the DC fold for a few years.

Mort Weisinger also made it a point to listen to fans and, if possible, give them what they wanted. He even had an answer to the unthinkable, whether *Lois Lane* would marry

Superman or *Superman* would die. For this he invented the 'imaginary' story which enabled him and DC to have their cake and eat it too. In later years it became overworked and irritating but early in the Silver Age some powerful stories were told in this way. The book-length *Death of Superman* was a perfect example. Recently it was included by popular choice of industry experts in the reprint volume The Greatest Superman Stories Ever Told.

If big things were happening in the first five years of the Silver Age at DC, what had been going on not too far away at the Marvel offices? Precisely nothing. In fact the company, once known as Timely Comics and still run by Martin Goodman, was not branded with any particular name in those days. But things were about to change.

Following the demise of the super-hero genre – which for Timely meant the end of *Captain America, The Human Torch, Sub-Mariner* and its other stars – Goodman's company had followed fashion, giving the public what it thought it wanted. Thus it provided crime and western comics in the late Forties and war comics in the early Fifties, followed by a line of CCA-compliant horror and science fiction titles. These included **Journey into Mystery, Strange Tales** and, later, **Tales of Suspense, Tales to Astonish** and **Amazing Adventures** (becoming **Amazing (Adult) Fantasy**).

Goodman became aware how well one of the new DC titles, **Justice League of America**, was selling and decided that his comics group should try something similar. He called in his main creative man who, besides being just about everything else in the pre-Marvel office, was also his cousin-in-law. This was Stan Lee, destined to be one of the most powerful influences on the modern comic book.

Lee had begun his career in comics as a seventeen-year-old working for Goodman's Timely. He was little more than an office boy at first, called upon to do just about anything; not very stimulating, perhaps, but first-rate experience. He graduated to writing stories for all of Timely's existing characters and created new ones too. By the Fifties Lee had become a creative force and the lynchpin of the business: he was principal script-writer and editor-in-chief.

Goodman probably expected Lee to come back with a pale imitation of **Justice League**. Instead, Jack Kirby, who had recently returned to the firm, collaborated with Lee to create a completely different team of superheroes called *The Fantastic Four*. They were led by Reed Richards, a scientist who had the power to elongate his body into

Showcase
No. 9 (August 1957)

The comic that began the Marvel Age of Comics,
The Fantastic Four
No. 1 (November 1961)

Tales to Astonish
No. 39 (January 1963)

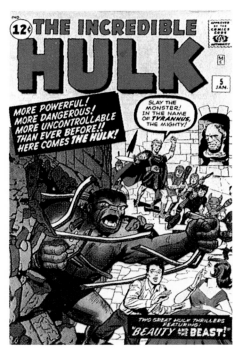

The Incredible Hulk
No. 5 (January 1963)

Strange Tales
No. 107 (April 1963)

Journey into Mystery
No. 89 (February 1962)

fantastic shapes (hence his name *Mr Fantastic),* and joined by his fiancée Sue Storm (who could turn invisible), her kid brother, Johnny *(The Human Torch)* and Ben Grimm, who was immensely strong with armour-plated orange skin and called *The Thing.*

The characters struck a nerve. In one bold move Lee accomplished for his heroes what it was taking Mort Weisinger an age to do with *Superman* over at DC: genuine three-dimensional characters. And that was exactly what Lee created

with many other major series he initiated in the next few years. After **The Fantastic Four** came **The Incredible Hulk,** a Jekyll and Hyde type tale of scientist Dr Bruce Banner who turned into the green-skinned brute of the title. Although this did not enjoy early success, in later years *The Hulk* became one of Marvel's most popular characters.

Other Marvel heroes came thick and fast in the early Sixties: **Journey into Mystery** Number 83 (August 1962) featured *Thor, God of Thunder. Ant Man* arrived in **Tales to Astonish**

Number 35 (September 1962); *The Human Torch* was given his own strip in **Strange Tales** Number 101 (October 1962) and, beginning in **Tales of Suspense** Number 39 (March 1963) there was *Iron Man,* a hero who depended on his unique armour both to stay alive and to fight villains.

All were popular, but the hero who really caught hold was *The Amazing Spider-Man.* Lee introduced the character in the last issue of **Amazing Fantasy** (Number 15) pulling out all the stops because, as it was

Daredevil
No. 1 (April 1964)

The Amazing Spider-Man
No. 1 (March 1963)

X-Men
No. 3 (January 1964)

Tales of Suspense
No. 45 (September 1963)

the final number, he felt he had nothing to lose. Here was an individual up to his ears in problems, who cared more about money than helping people, and who was riddled with insecurity. His alter-ego was an unimpressive teenager named Peter Parker.

Spider-Man was written by Stan Lee and drawn by Steve Ditko, an artist deliberately chosen by Lee for his understated art. Sales for that final issue of **Amazing Fantasy** and letters arriving at the publisher's offices resulted in **The Amazing Spider-Man** Number 1 (March 1963). And almost immediately it became as popular as **The Fantastic Four,** if not more so.

Following the DC example, Lee also started reviving his company's old heroes from the Forties: besides *The Human Torch,* there soon appeared *Captain America* and the *Sub-Mariner,* both of whom became hugely popular. So, too, did new heroes like the highly original *Daredevil,* a blind man whose extra-sensory abilities gave him extraordinary powers; and the *X-Men,* a group of

teenage mutants. But perhaps Stan Lee and Jack Kirby's finest creation was a character introduced in a long-running **Fantastic Four** tale in the mid-Sixties: the *Silver Surfer,* herald of *Galactus,* a world-devouring giant.

Marvel was no less creative with its super-villains and foes, creating as many eccentrics and flawed individuals as heroes. The company and its products made a deep and lasting impression on the whole of the comics industry in the Sixties. The effects are still with us. For some it was the Silver Age of comics but Stan Lee and his fellow creators applied a more accurate epithet: it was also the Marvel Age of comics.

New trends

By 1970 the big boom was over and Marvel and DC inevitably lost much of the innovative impetus that had driven them through the previous decade. As formulae scripts tended to become the norm, superhero popularity waned and monthlies such as **Conan the Barbarian** (Marvel: October 1970) and **Swamp Thing** (DC: October 1972) found favour with readers, adding a new originality and some splendid supporting art.

Jack Kirby's arrival at DC Comics, after leaving Marvel, gave cause for some excitement as DC allowed him complete creative control. He wrote and drew **The New Gods** (February 1971), **Forever People** (February 1971), **Mr Miracle** (March 1971), **The Demon** (August 1972) and **Kamandi** (October 1972) as well as **Superman's Pal Jimmy Olsen**. But despite his splendid art, the lack of Stan Lee's scripts was noticeable and the books suffered as a result.

During the Seventies and Eighties the comics industry experienced several different vogues. The Golden Age and Silver Age had seemingly exhausted all the potential superpowers and gimmicks. Genuinely new heroes therefore were few and far between and, generally speaking, second division. Of special note, however, were stars like *The Creeper* (drawn by Steve Ditko and written by Denny O'Neil) and *Deadman* (drawn by Neil Adams and scripted by various writers), both for DC Comics. In both cases it was the quality of the art and innovative writing that made them a success with comics fans.

One still very popular comics genre was war. The first title dedicated entirely to this was **War Comics** (Dell: May 1940); and the fight against the Germans and Japanese was a recurring theme in the superhero comics until the mid-Forties.

Conan the Barbarian
No. 1 (October 1970)

In the Fifties different publishers issued titles about the Korean war, with DC's **Two-Fisted Tales** and **Frontline Combat** proving the most successful. In August 1952 DC launched three war titles: **All American Men of War**, **Our Army at War** and **Star Spangled War Stories**. Later, **Our Fighting Forces** (October 1954) and **GI Combat** (January 1957) were added to the line-up.

DC, more successfully than any other company before or since, made stars of its soldiers. Writer and editor Robert Kanigher provided superb characterizations for creations such as *Sgt Rock of Easy Company, Gunner and Sarge,* and *Johnny Cloud, the Navaho Air Ace.* Additional original touches were offered in the form of a haunted tank, commanded by a Civil War general in a continuing series called *The Haunted Tank*, and a different angle on the First World War when it was seen from the other side's point of view in *Enemy Ace*.

Kanigher's stories were lifted to the peak of excellence by the superior

artwork of one draftsman in particular: Joe Kubert. His action, artistry and sheer professionalism graced features like *Sgt Rock* and *Enemy Ace* with unparalleled realism. Kubert's powerful art was full of interesting and dramatic angles. Anatomically correct and realistic, his figures were heavily shaded, and the effect made his work superbly atmospheric.

Joe Kubert eventually succeeded Robert Kanigher as editor of DC's war comics, allowing Kanigher to devote more time to his writing. The result was the continuing popularity of DC's war line, a popularity which lasted until the late Eighties.

Marvel's incursion into the theatre of war was the immensely readable, if over-the-top, **Sgt Fury and His Howling Commandos** (May 1963). No realism here, just wisecracking Marvel action all the way as a bunch of eclectic individuals, led by a cigar-chomping sergeant, handled 'impossible' missions to defeat the Nazis during an eighteen-year run. A spin-off, **Captain Savage and His**

Sgt Fury and His Howling Commandos *No. 1 (May 1963)*

Leatherneck Raiders, was not so successful, expiring after less than two years.

Twenty-three years later, in 1986, Marvel succeeded in introducing a little more realism with **The 'Nam**, an account of the conflict in Vietnam. The war genre peaked long ago but no doubt it will be back. By the time this appears in print there will, no doubt, be more than one title featuring the recent war in the Gulf. As long as man wages war, comics will be bound to feature it.

By the late Seventies comics fans formed a large and powerful grouping which was beginning to influence the comics industry at all levels. The movement had its origins in 1961 when enthusiast Jerry Bails and another fan, Roy Thomas, had produced the first comics fanzine, **Alter Ego**. It became very popular and helped to kick-start the concept of fandom, inspiring others to produce their own magazines. Bails went on to organize comic book conventions and produce valuable reference works. Thomas was

one of the first fans to break into the business, becoming an important scriptwriter for DC and Marvel.

Some fans turned out to be talented businessmen. Former high-school teacher Phil Sueling opened up his specialist retail comic shop in 1969. Frustrated by the currently established distribution system for comics, he started up his own. Its success influenced others to do the same. One in particular was Bud Plant, a young fan who, with his partner John Barrett, established a small chain of direct sales comic shops. Plant then went on to create a national distribution service to the ever-increasing number of specialist shops that were opening across the United States.

Fans became older. Once, they had stopped reading comics when they reached sixteen or so, but by the Seventies many were in their twenties, thirties or even forties. This had a major impact on the industry — particularly in the writing of the stories. Writers now strove — and many succeeded — to achieve both real-

ism and relevance. The industry began to mature rapidly. New independent publishers appeared and, in certain instances, challenged the established giants Marvel and DC.

Some of these were writers and artists who wished to retain ownership of their creations and who had started their own publications. Others were companies who had no wish to abide by the Comics Code, seeing it as an overt form of censorship or simply as a shackle on their creativity. But as the Fifties became more distant, changing times made the Code less relevant than before. Even big publishers were not averse to issuing material without the CCA stamp — something they might not have been able to do were it not for the system of direct distribution and the hundreds of specialist shops.

DC made the two most significant contributions to comics of the 1980s. First there was **Batman: The Dark Knight Returns** (March 1986) by Frank Miller. It featured an ageing, almost unrecognizable Batman, paired with a female Robin, roaming a Gotham City that was a blend between Hell and Fritz Lang's *Metropolis*. Secondly, there was the twelve-issue **Watchmen** series written by Alan Moore and drawn by Dave Gibbons. Complex, mature and without visual gimmickry, it broke new ground for the industry and is certain to have an effect on the direction of comics as a whole.

In recent years DC has also retained the initiative by revamping the most popular of its heroes: *Superman, The Flash, Green Lantern* and consequently, the *Justice League*. This has been largely successful, giving cause for fans to hope that a new age of comics may be dawning. History shall judge what will be its nature — Gold, Silver, Platinum or otherwise — but it is clear that in the United States comics will in the next decade be as varied and interesting as they have been in the last ten.

4ᵉ ANNÉE. — N° 52   1O Centimes   25 DÉCEMBRE 1895

Le Pêle-Mêle

JOURNAL HUMORISTIQUE HEBDOMADAIRE

POUR TOUS
ET
PAR TOUS

ABONNEMENTS
FRANCE : UN AN . 6 fr. SIX MOIS : 3 fr. 50
ÉTRANGER : UN AN . 9 fr. SIX MOIS : 5 fr. »

ON S'ABONNE DANS TOUS LES BUREAUX DE POSTE

PARIS
7 — Rue Cadet — 7

LES MANUSCRITS NE SONT PAS RENDUS

Tous les articles insérés restent la propriété du journal. — La reproduction en est interdite à tous ceux qui n'ont pas de traité avec le Pêle-Mêle.

EUROPEAN COMICS

Au milieu du détroit, le paquebot saute, et le Télescope est lancé à une hauteur prodigieuse.

L'astronome Apogée, savant Ginvernois, qui se promène à l'œil nu dans son jardin aperçoit le nouveau corps céleste.

Les vingt huit observateurs salariés qu'il emploie à regarder le ciel jour et nuit l'aperçoivent pareillement.

Rodolphe Töpffer's Le Docteur Festus *shows his fresh and vibrant approach in weaving exceptional graphic narratives around humorous and clever texts. This picture story was in* **Histoires en Etampes** *in 1846*

First published in book form in 1865 Wilhelm Busch's Max und Moritz *was one of the most influential picture-stories in the history of comics*

Europe dominated the earliest days of the comic strip until the early 1900s. Indeed it was the Swiss author and educator Rodolphe Töpffer (1799-1846) who is often credited with developing the first true comic strips. By making brilliant use of his limited drawing ability, he created a type of shorthand picture-writing and demonstrated 'cinematic' story-telling techniques a half century before cinema came into being.

Töpffer's elliptical style, a result of his poor eyesight, caught the attention of Goethe who was instrumental in convincing the artist to publish his stories. Töpffer's eight 'dramas-in-pictures' included *Les Amours de M. Vieuxbois, Les Voyages et Aventures de Docteur Festus, Monsieur Cryptogramme, Histoire de M. Jabot, La Veritable Histoire de M. Crepin, L'Histoire d'Albert, Monsieur Pencil* and *L'Histoire de*

Jacques. These were collected in **Histoires en Etampes** (Stories in Etchings) in 1846, a landmark in the history of comics.

In 1847 the German artist and writer Heinrich Hoffmann had published the first edition of his **Struwwelpeter** (Shock-headed Peter), an anthology of admonitory anecdotes concerning delinquent infants, which was to have a far-reaching influence on comic strips through to the present day. By replacing cherubic or heroic young adventurers with diabolical children characterized by reprehensible behaviour, Hoffmann set a trend which was to recur in countless children's strips

Heinrich Hoffman's ever popular **Struwwelpeter** was published in Germany in 1847 and by 1848 had reached the shores of England where he is still a firm favourite

An early picture-story by Wilhelm Busch for **Bilderbogen** entitled The Transformation, this forerunner of the comic strip aptly displays Busch's biting wit and inspired line

and influence cartoonists from Edward Lear to Wilhelm Busch to Rudolph Dirks.

Töpffer's and Hoffman's works inspired another generation of European artists, including Gustave Doré, Caran d'Ache and, most notably with regard to the comics field, the aforementioned Wilhelm Busch (1832-1908).

Busch was a German artist, poet and cartoonist whose contributions to the weekly **Fliegenden Blätter** and **Bilderbogen** rank among the finest and earliest comic work. The most famous of his picture-stories was undoubtedly *Max und Moritz* (1865), a story told in cartoons and verse about two malevolent young pranksters. Although it was cri-

Wilhelm Busch's Max und Moritz *prepare to steal the Widow Bolte's chickens in yet another prank which led to their eventual gruesome come-uppance*

ticized in its day by pedagogues because of its grim moral, *Max und Moritz* has become a children's classic and a proven cornerstone in the field of comics.

Ironically, *Max und Moritz* had a larger influence on the development of the American comic strip than it did in its own country. When it was translated in 1871 and published in the United States, it became the inspiration for *The Katzenjammer Kids*, one of the most popular comic strips of all time.

In Germany, however, despite the wit, social satire and biting sarcasm of Busch's work, comic strips remained 'kid's stuff' until the late 1960s and failed to attain the adult readership that was achieved elsewhere. Their development stagnated as most cartoonists continued to ignore the use of word-balloons until the 1940s, prolonging the tradition of stories-in-verse long after it was due to be replaced.

In France, as in Germany, the nineteenth century brought a flourish of illustrated narratives which appeared in publications such as **Images d'Epinal** which catered, quite intentionally, for the more vulgar public tastes. One of France's earliest strip pioneers was Georges Colomb (1856-1945), an artist, writer and professor of natural science who contributed to various illustrated magazines under the penname of 'Christophe'.

Christophe's most notable comic work appeared in the weekly **Le Petit Français Illustré** where his *La Famille Fenouillard* commenced in 1889. This was considered by many to be the first French comic feature to have reached such a wide public, although, on a par with attitudes towards comics throughout Europe, it appealed almost exclusively to children.

In common with Busch, Colomb's picture stories also relied on text without word-balloons. His stylistic innovations, utilizing odd angles and accelerated narratives, placed his work years ahead of its time and he exercised a particularly strong influence on the content and structure of other French picture stories.

Colomb produced further notable comic work including *Les Facéties du Sapper Camember* in 1890 and

A typical example of turn-of-the-century French humour magazines, the 1898 Christmas issue of **Le Pêle-Mêle** *boasted a cover by Benjamin Rabier*

the picture-story *L'Idée Fixe du Savant Cosinus* which ran in **Le Petit Français Illustré** from 1893 to 1897 before he abandoned the comic field altogether to devote himself to an academic career.

After the turn of the century the Americans were striding forcefully ahead with numerous newspaper strips and Sunday comics by superb artists, appealing to both children and adults. The Europeans were left in their wake, despite the flourishing of talented cartoonists in a profusion of humour and satirical

magazines like France's **La Plume, Cocorico, Le Rire, Le Canard Sauvage** and, most notably, **L'Assiette au Beurre**. Painters such as Juan Gris (José Victoriano González), Franz Kupka and Kees Van Dongen all contributed worthy cartoons but none bridged the gap into the comics field.

Although there was no major comics tradition established in Europe during the first two decades of the 1900s, there were several publications which offered a venue for reprints of American strips as well

A *humour strip by Marcel Capy for issue number 52 of* **Le Pêle Mêle**

Lanched in 1924 in **Le Petit Illustré**, *Louis Forton's* Bibi Fricotin *was a long-running feature of great inventiveness*

that its political allusions had been aimed primarily at adults.

Forton (1879-1934), an inveterate gambler and bon vivant, was a major influence on many French cartoonists of the time and helped to establish France as a major centre of comic strip creation in years to come. His other contributions included the military strip *La Carrière Militaire d'Onésime Baluchon* in 1909, *Les Cent Vingt-Six Métiers de Caramel,* about a born loser, in 1920, and the autobiographical *Bibi Fricotin*, his second most popular strip, in 1924.

American reprints had started to reach Europe by 1906 and Denmark's **Hjemmet** was one of the first weekly magazines to publish translations. In its pages *Buster Brown* became *Lile Svends Gavtyvestrger* (Little Svend's Pranks) and *The Katzenjammer Kids* appeared under the title *Knold og Tot* in 1908. These early imports laid the foundations for Bulls Presstjänst, which became one of the largest comics and features syndicates in Europe, drawing much of its material from America's King Features Syndicate.

as original picture-stories: in 1902 the French magazine **Le Jeudi de la Jeunesse** began publication, followed by the comic weekly **L'Illustré** (which later became known as **Le Petit Illustré**) in 1904.

Several popular strips with text evolved including **La Semaine De Suzette's** *Bécassine* by Pinchon and Camery in 1905, and cartoonist Louis Forton's most famous creation, the scurrilous *La Bande des Pieds-Nickelés* (The Nickel-Plated-Feet Gang) in 1908. The latter series appeared in issue Number 9 of the newly established French children's weekly, **L'Epatant,** despite the fact

Louis Forton's classic La Bande des Pieds-Nickelés *appeared in* **L'Épatant** *from 1908. It enabled Forton to swipe at established institutions and personalities with barbed wit and expertly aimed jibes. The exploits of this band of swindlers and con-artists became a national institution in France*

Bilbolbul and Bonaventura

Italy was one of the few European countries to make any innovative progress with comic strips before the 1920s. 1908 saw the introduction of a weekly supplement of the daily newspaper **Corriere della Sera**. Entitled **Il Corriere dei Piccoli**, the first issue contained a pioneering strip by artist Attilio Mussino, *Bilbolbul*.

Illustrations for the imaginative, paradoxical and metaphoric *Bilbolbul* were accompanied by verse captions recounting the crimes and punishments of a stereotyped black savage boy in an imaginary Africa where everything was taken literally and turned into pictures.

Unfortunately, *Bilbolbul*'s visual transformations frightened children as well as fascinating them and the strip was cancelled in 1912.

Italy's most beloved cartoon character, Sergio Tofano's Il Signor Bonaventura, *delighted readers for more than half a century and inspired two theatre adaptations and a 1942 film*

Mussino was directed to turn his creative impulses to more sedate strips, one of which was a short-lived imitation of *Little Nemo*, but none had the impact or popularity of *Bilbolbul*.

Il Corriere dei Piccoli nevertheless went from strength to strength and was soon the most successful Italian publication for children. The combined efforts of artists such as Mussino and Antonio Rubino (1880-1964) assured that the pages were filled with a myriad of new creations, alongside reprints of American strips including *Fortunello (Happy Hooligan)*, *Bibi e Bibo (The Katzenjammer Kids)* and *Arcibaldo e Petronilla (Bringing up Father)*. It was Rubino's idea that the speech-balloons in these strips be replaced with captions in verse, thus bringing the American strips in line with the Italian tradition.

Rubino served on **Il Corriere dei Piccoli** for two decades, performing both editorial and artistic duties. He was a major contributor and creator for the weekly, his most famous strip being *Quadratino* (Little Square Head) which first appeared

in 1910 and ran until 1940. His style was a combination of geometric design and floral pattern which, embellished by his mastery of colour and his sinuous line, created imagery akin to Art Nouveau.

Il Corriere dei Piccoli continued to exert its influence on the Italian comic-reading public with the inclusion of *Il Signor Bonaventura*, a strip created by playwright, interpreter and cartoonist Sergio Tofano ('Sto') in 1917. The whimsical stories, executed in Tofano's simple line, ran for over fifty years and *Bonaventura* became one of the most popular and celebrated characters in Italian comics, so much so that he was revived in 1970 after a fifteen-year absence.

Tofano continued to draw the dapper character until his death in 1973 when *Bonaventura* was taken over by Carlo Peroni. The theme throughout centred on the optimism and ultimate rewards of a character wandering in search of good deeds to perform; no matter how great the calamities to befall him, *Bonaventura* always reaped a generous financial reward for his troubles.

The Triumph of Tintin

The 1920s and 1930s brought a new impetus to the comics of Europe. In 1921 Holland was introduced to its first successful daily newspaper strip in the form of *Bulletje en Bonestaak* (Fatty and Beanstalk) written by Adrianus Michael de Jong and drawn by George van Raemdonck in a down-to-earth and realistic style. As with most European strips of the first half of this century, *Bulletje en Bonestaak* was about the adventures of children – the Europeans preferred these to animal strips or family strips. Appearing in the newspaper **Het Volk**, the strip ran until 1934 and inspired a long series of reprint book editions between 1924 and the present day.

By the mid-1920s, Louis Forton was already established as one of France's leading comic artists, and American imports such as *The Gumps* were appearing in French children's publications. Then in 1925 one of the most important and influential comic strips of Europe was created by the French cartoonist, journalist and writer, Alain Saint-Ogan (1895-1974). His first comic strip *Zig et Puce*, about two venturesome youngsters, appeared in the weekly **Dimanche Illustré** and heralded the introduction of the Art Deco look to the comic-strip field. It was also the first French comic feature to make use of the word-balloon exclusively.

In 1926 Saint-Ogan added the famous mascot, the penguin Alfred, and *Zig et Puce* ran in a variety of publications until the late 1960s, having been drawn by Saint-Ogan until 1963. Its immediate success in 1925 prompted Saint-Ogan to create a number of other comic features including *Mitou et Toti* in 1932, *Prosper l'Ours* in 1933 and *Monsieur Poche* in 1934.

Bulletje en Bonestaak *(Fatty and Beanstalk), ran in Holland's* **Het Volk** *from 1921 until 1934. Here the two boys visit the* **London Evening News***while journeying around the world and encounter Jopie Slim and Dikkie Bigmans, strip stars of the English paper*

The star attraction of the French weekly **Dimanche Illustré** *from 1925 to 1937,* Zig et Puce, *as drawn by Alain Saint-Ogan, told the worldwide adventures of two young boys, their mascot penguin Alfred, and the young American heiress, Dolly. After 1937, the strip continued in various publications until the 1960s*

Tintin, Captain Haddock and Snowy on the trail of more adventures in **The Calculus Affair** *from 1956*

Dated 13 August 1924, issue No. 33 of Denmark's **Illustreret-Familie-Journal** *boasted a bumper 40 pages of interesting and educational articles, anecdotes and adventure stories. Also included were reprinted British comic strips* Pitch & Toss, Basil and Bert *(for once in splendid colour) and* Rob the Rover

The influence of Saint-Ogan's style stretched far and wide. The most famous of all European cartoonists, the Belgian Georges Rémi (known to one and all as Hergé, creator of *Tintin*), owed his cartooning début to Saint-Ogan. After creating *Totor de la Patrouille des Hannetons* (Totor of the June Bug Patrol) for a boy-scout paper in 1926, Hergé was encouraged by Saint-Ogan to create *Tintin* for the weekly supplement of the Belgian daily **Le Vingtième Siècle** in 1929. *Tintin* books began to appear in 1930 and more than twenty-one full-length adventures were published over the next forty-six years, the last being *Tintin et les Picaros* in 1976.

With his quiff of red hair and his faithful dog companion *Milou* (Snowy), *Tintin* became the quintessential European comic character of the century. Despite his enormous popularity on one side of the Atlantic, he never fully caught on in America; yet the influence of Hergé in Europe was immense and a whole school of cartooning grew up around him, known as 'the Brussels school', which eventually spearheaded the post-war renaissance of European comic art.

There were few other noteworthy indigenous European strips to appear in the 1920s, but of particular merit was Spain's *Macaco* strip, created in 1928 by K-Hito (Ricardo Garcia Lopez) as the star attraction of the weekly comic magazine to which it gave its name. Utilizing a clean and simple graphic style, sparse text to accentuate the action and a skilful use of colour, K-Hito created a surrealistic universe inhabited by *Macaco*, a little man with an inclination for rest and sleep, and his young brother *Macaquete*.

Throughout the 1920s and 1930s, various British strips were imported to countries such as Denmark where, for example, *Rob the Rover* appeared weekly, renamed *Willy*, in

Alfred Bestall's Rupert and the Strange Airman *as it appeared in the Dutch newspaper* **Algemeen Handelsblad** *on 31 January 1938*

the **Illustreret Familie-Journal**, and strips by one of Britain's finest comic artists, Roy Wilson, were reprinted in various newspapers. These included *Basil and Bert* and *Pitch and Toss*, two of Britain's most popular series.

In Holland, the newspaper **Algemeen Handelsblad** ran the ever-popular Mary Tourtel and Alfred Bestall *Rupert* panels which they also reprinted in paperback book form for many years. *Bruintje Beer*, as he was known to Dutch children, became a firm favourite, widely collected in Holland to this day.

The 1930s brought a revolution in American comic strips which was echoed in the European field: the introduction of the 'adventure strip' overwhelmed the fledgling competition from the European comic-

producing countries. *Popeye, Dick Tracy, Mickey Mouse, Tarzan* and *Terry and the Pirates* were the order of the day and the American syndicates inundated Europe with their enormous output.

Few original strips in the European tradition appeared during the decade. Switzerland came up with *Globi*, a comic character who grew out of an advertising campaign for the Swiss department store Globus. Created by J.K. Schiele and Robert Lips in 1932, *Globi* soon had his own magazine, **Der Globi**, which appeared monthly from 1935. *Globi* books were published worldwide for the next forty years and proved tremendously popular in France, Belgium and Holland as well as post-war Germany and Austria.

In 1934 the first French daily newspaper strip appeared entitled *Les Aventures de Professeur Nimbus* by A. Daix. Also at that time the **Journal de Mickey**, containing reprints, commenced publication.

In the same year Germany produced the original humour strip *Vater und Sohn* (Father and Son) by Erich Ohser under the pseudonym E.O. Plauen, which was reprinted all over the world. Millions of readers followed the pranks and adventures in this quietly witty 'pantomime' strip that only used words for subtitles. Ironically, after creating such a much-loved source of humour and gentleness, Ohser was eventually driven to commit suicide in 1944 after his arrest by the Gestapo for alleged 'defeatist remarks in an air-raid shelter'.

The Spanish, Italians and French made an effort to keep up with the Americans by introducing their own adventure strips. In 1935 Jesús Blascu originated *Cuto* in Spain's comic magazine **Boliche**. Although the boy hero's adventures were soon discontinued, Blascu revived the character in 1940 and *Cuto* went

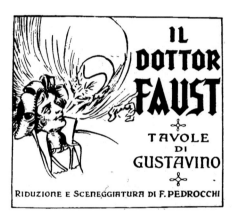

Cuto rescues the damsel in distress in a perilous adventure devised by Spanish artist Jesús Blascu

Gustavo Rosso was the first artist to draw Il Dottor Faust *in 1939. As well as escaping Italy's strict censorship due to its high moral tone, the strip served as a propaganda link with Italy's war-time ally, Germany*

on to become one of Spain's most popular comic strips, appearing first in the comic weekly **Chicos** and later, from 1974, in **Chito**. It also appeared in Portugal's **Jornal do Cuto** from 1973.

In Italy in 1937 the Italians began to create their own adventure strips: *Kit Carson* by Rino Albertarelli was the first Italian Western comic strip, appearing in **Topolino** until 1938, and it became a classic of the Golden Age of Italian comics; *Gino e Gianni*, based on Lyman Young's *Tim Tyler's Luck*, was another masterpiece of an adventure strip, again

Tom Poes and friends go for a jolly walkabout in Marten Toonder's splendid painting for **Tom Puss Tales**, *a book printed and published in England containing stories of the white cat's adventures*

few American imports were received. In France, for example, the magazine **Tarzan** appeared in 1941 but was soon discontinued because of its alleged immorality and its American influences. French substitutes for the American comics included **Le Téméraire**, **Sirocco** and **Fanfan la Tulipe**.

Even some of the most popular original European strips failed to see out the war. In 1938 Dutch writer and artist Marten Toonder created *Tom Poes* (Tom Puss) which, after having been published successfully in foreign newspapers for several years, began appearing at home in 1941 as a daily strip in the Dutch newspaper **De Telegraaf**, only to be suspended in 1944 for the duration of the war. It was reinstated in 1947 and went on to become phenomenally popular not only in the Netherlands but worldwide.

Tom Poes, the adventures of a cuddly cat, was not Toonder's only success: *Tobias* (1931), *Brahm Ibrahim* (1932), *Uk en Puk* (1934), *Japie Makreel* (1940), *Kappie* (1946), *Panda* (1946), *Koning Hollewijn* (1954) and numerous other strips have made Toonder the most influential Dutch cartoonist of the century. In 1942 he founded the Marten Toonder Studios to produce both cartoons and comic strips which appeared in more than fifteen countries.

Hergé's *Tintin*, like *Rupert* in England, appeared throughout the 1940s despite the wartime shortages. The **Tintin** magazine was published for the first time in Belgium in 1946 and in the same

beautifully rendered by Albertarelli for **Topolino**; and *Il Dottor Faust*, adapted from Wolfgang Goethe's masterpiece of German literature, was yet another remarkable Italian comic strip achievement drawn at first by Gustavo Rosso in 1939 for the comic weekly **L'Audace**, and then revived brilliantly by Albertarelli for **Topolino** in 1941.

The Italians certainly excelled at the adventure strip, aided to some extent by their Fascist regime's ban on the import of American material immediately prior to the onset of the Second World War. Mondadori's weeklies **Topolino** and **Paperino** were large-circulation venues for a

wealth of original Italian efforts, including *Romano il Legionario* and *Dick Fulmine*, all inspired by the sudden lack of American strips.

In Germany, however, the effect of the war and national isolationism resulted in a comic vacuum that persisted until the post-war years. Satire had ceased in 1933 and virtually no new strips evolved during the 1940s, for Hitler despised the comic medium.

Throughout the rest of Europe both the wartime paper shortages and the embargoes on non-essential imports took their toll as less space was available for comic strips and

year it appeared in Holland under the title of **Kuifje**.

Belgium's **Spirou** magazine had begun publication in 1938 and, along with the French periodicals **Coq Hardi** and **Vaillant**, both commencing in 1946, it was dramatically influenced by the style and

format of the **Tintin** magazine when it first appeared in that year.

Also in 1946, the Belgian cartoonist Maurice de Bevère created the long-running humorous western strip *Lucky Luke*, which began appearing in **Spirou** in 1947 under de Bevère's pen-name Morris. The strip, with its lonesome eponymous cowboy hero bringing justice to the Wild West

before riding off into the sunset of each episode, was an instant success. *Lucky Luke* often incorporated authentic famous characters from the Wild West. In 1955 de Bevère began collaborating with French writer and editor René Goscinny of *Asterix* fame. The strip was transferred to the French magazine **Pilote** in 1968 — a joint venture in which Goscinny served as editor-in-chief.

Lucky Luke, the 'poor lonesome cowboy', makes an impact at the local saloon

Post-war revival

By 1948, the American comics were beginning to reappear in Europe. German newspapers once again carried translations and a number of reprint paperbacks began to filter on to the market. In France, however, there emerged a strong opposition to the spread of American strips in the country. Attacked because they threatened the national spirit as well as providing unwanted competition for the French artists and writers, the American imports came under the scrutiny of a control board set up in 1949 to supervise French comic production rigorously.

Thus indigenous comics finally established themselves in France and in French-speaking countries. Their marketing was linked with media tie-ins such as television shows and animated films, giving them a far-reaching popularity. Throughout the 1950s, the comic industry of Europe developed without the overpowering influence of the Americans, and so established its own position in the world history of comics.

But one major intruder did manage to make his presence felt: Walt Disney's *Mickey Mouse* landed in Europe to resounding success. In Germany he appeared in 1951 in the monthly **Micky Maus** and by 1957 his popularity had grown to warrant weekly publications. While American superheroes came and went with a general lack of enduring success, the German public welcomed *Micky* and his pals with open arms.

In the 1950s the Germans followed the American and French examples with a campaign against violence in comics which they termed 'Books for Young People in Exchange for Rubbish'. However, as most of the 'objectionable' American material had never reached Germany in the first place, the movement had little

Clean-cut auto racer Michel Vaillant brought fame to cartoonist Jean Graton when he first appeared in Tintin *magazine in 1957*

to do and the more innocuous imports from the rest of Europe and from America continued to prosper.

Comics such as **Yabu, Wild West** and **Der Fidele Cowboy** (The Faithful Cowboy) had long runs in Germany, as did **Tarzan, Pecos Bill** and **Der Kleine Sheriff** (The Little Sheriff), although most strips were censored, with text replacing any 'violent' sequences with knives or pistols.

Sigurd, created by Hansrudi Wascher and published weekly from 1953 by Walter Lehning, was one of the few genuine German comic books of the period. With a blond knight errant as its hero, **Sigurd** appeared in the Italian *piccolo* format and was the most popular of the Walter Lehning line of uniquely German entries in the roll-call of comic history.

1953 also brought the début of Rolf Kauka's **Fix und Foxi** which had previously appeared in Germany as **Eulenspiegel** in 1952. The comic was second in popularity only to Disney's **Micky Maus** and consisted of comedy adventures built around two clever little foxes. The strip spawned a host of merchandising: dolls, puppets, cups, puzzles, calendars, T-shirts and a 1972 cartoon all contributing to the comic's long-running popularity.

The Belgians continued to be at the forefront of European comic invention following the success of their **Tintin** and **Spirou** magazines in the

Edgar P. Jacobs's best-selling characters Blake et Mortimer *are popular stars of a thriller serial based in London. They have inspired radio plays and records, and plans for a live-action film of their exploits await realization*

1940s. In 1954 cartoonist Peyo (Pierre Culliford) joined **Spirou**, bringing with him his strip *Johan et Pirlouit* which he had created in 1947. From this strip evolved one of Belgium's most popular worldwide exports: *The Smurfs*.

Originally appearing as *Les Schtroumpfs* in *Johan et Pirlouit* in 1957, the endearing race of elves were given their own strip in 1960. Again the media link-up that the Europeans had perfected was all-important: toys, books, television series and animated films ensured that *The Schtroumpfs* reached the widest possible audience.

Other inspirational Belgian post-war strips included Willy Vandersteen's long-running *Suske en Wiske* (1945), Edgar P. Jacobs's brilliant science-fiction strip *Blake et Mortimer* (appearing in **Tintin** from 1946) and Jacques Martin's Roman Empire tale, *Alix l'Intrépide* (appearing in **Tintin** from 1948).

Belgium also excelled in realistic adventure stories, with strips like *Ric Hochet*, created in 1955 by cartoonist Tibet (Gilbert Gascard) and writer André-Paul Duchâteau for **Tintin**. A superior police strip with suspenseful action, *Ric Hochet* became one of the most successful contemporary European strips.

Hard on its heels came Belgian cartoonist Jean Graton's auto-racing series called *Michel Vaillant* which appeared in **Tintin** as a regular feature from 1958. Exported near and far, the strip achieved phenomenal success considering the unexpressive artwork utilized on *Vaillant* and his racing team. But although his faces were flat and vacant, Graton managed to inject his cars with an excitement and verve that brought resounding success, especially in Germany where the strip appeared as *Michael Voss*.

Asterix sets the pace

France had many triumphs, too, including its fast-paced aviation strip, *Michel Tanguy*, which was created by writer Jean-Michel Charlier and illustrator Albert Uderzo for the first issue of **Pilote** in 1959. And in that same issue also appeared one of the most famous strips ever to come out of Europe, *Astérix le Gaulois*, also drawn by Uderzo but written by the cofounder of **Pilote**, René Goscinny.

Short of stature, but with a most impressive moustache, *Asterix* and friends *Obelix* the muscle-man and *Getafix the Druid* transformed their creators into multi-millionaires. Books, films, radio appearances, toys, games and computer software have succeeded in spreading the legend of *Asterix* around the world.

It is not surprising that *Asterix* was somewhat reminiscent of the classic US **Mad** comics of the 1950s, as

Jesús Blascu's Los Guerilleros *was created for the Belgian magazine* Spirou *but the trio of Western adventurers soon fought their way into the pages of a number of Spanish comics*

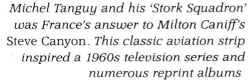

Michel Tanguy and his 'Stork Squadron' was France's answer to Milton Caniff's Steve Canyon. This classic aviation strip inspired a 1960s television series and numerous reprint albums

Asterix the Gaul, *created by René Goscinny and Albert Uderzo in 1959, has become world famous despite its chauvinistic brand of humour*

Goscinny had spent some time working with **Mad** creator, Harvey Kurtzman, at the EC shop in New York before returning to Europe with Maurice de Bevère in 1955 to collaborate on *Lucky Luke*. However, despite its phenomenal popularity in Europe during the 1960s, there were many who found the xenophobic superiority of the *Asterix* scripts over-bearing and tiresome; certainly *Asterix* never achieved such great success in the US, although he is still widely read in Europe today.

The comics of Spain were dominated by the three Blascu brothers, Jesús, Alejondra and Adriano, who joined together to produce Western comics for the French, English, Belgian, Portuguese and Spanish markets. Titles included **Billy the Kid, Wyatt Earp, Buffalo Bill, Blackbow** and **Shot Basky**. Jesús Blascu of *Cuto* fame became Spain's most prolific and accomplished comic artist, creating strips such as *Los Guerilleros* (in **Spirou, Chito** and so on from 1968), *Miss Tarantula, Montezuma's Daughter, The Inde-*structible Man, Phantom of the Forest* and *The Steel Claw*.

The Western strip has always been a firm favourite in Spain, with fine examples in the form of Francisco Batet's *El Coyote* (1946), Carlos Giménez's *Gringo* (1963) and Antonio Hernandez Palacio's *Manos Kelly* (1970).

In post-war Italy, a new format for comic books ushered in a wave of increased circulation. Regular comics were replaced by small 'strip books' or 'pocket books' which became known as the *piccolo* format. These were exported widely throughout Europe and found an especially huge audience in Germany where they were published by Lehning Verlag.

A French version of Sciuscia *published post-World War II*

Francisco Batet's El Coyote *recounted the tales of a Zorro-style avenger and became one of Spain's most popular comics during the late 1940s*

One Italian publisher who was notably successful with the *piccolo* comics was Tristano Torelli whose first success was with **Sciuscia** (Shoeshine Boy), followed by **Il Piccolo Sceriffo** (The Little Sheriff) in 1950. The latter was the story of young Kit who replaced his father as sheriff after he had been killed by outlaws. Kit proceeded to bring law and order to the Wild West for more than twenty years.

While many of the post-war Italian comics were home-made products such as **Akim, El Carnera, Pecos Bill, Il Piccolo Sceriffo** or **Il Piccolo Ranger**, the American imports also made their mark. *Mickey Mouse and Company* was distributed under the title **Topolino** and *Superman* was widely read as *Nembo Kid*. (He did not regain his real name until 1966.)

All of Italy's comics appeared in a wide variety of formats but the *piccolo* variety was certainly one of the most popular during the fifteen years or so that it prevailed.

The 1956 version of Pecos Bill *as drawn by Pietro Gamba. The strip originated in 1949 and rekindled the Italian love of Westerns after the war-time lull*

The comics come of age

The late 1960s heralded a new era in European comics. Inspired by the imports of American Underground Comics, the Europeans proceeded to make the 'adult comic' their own, producing sophisticated, elegantly rendered strips for an entirely new age group. European comics grew up, burying for ever the outdated notion that their predecessors had adhered to so stringently — that comics were only for children.

Before the onslaught of the adult comics, however, in the first half of the decade, the French comics, known as *Bandes Dessinées*, or BDs for short, were already beginning to appeal to an older age group and to receive deserved attention. In 1962 the first French comics club, Le Club des Bandes Dessinées, was launched, indicating the increasing seriousness with which comics were being regarded. In that same year, Jean-Claude Forest created the sex-cum-science-fiction strip

Barbarella; this strip exposed the titillating adventures of a beautiful and sex-loving astronaut, and appeared in **V-Magazine**.

Barbarella rocked the comic establishment with her sexual exploits, so much so that the book version of her adventures was banned by the French authorities. However, her appearance cleared the way for further risqué strips to follow in response to the overwhelming popular appeal that she generated.

Cocco Bill *by Benito Jacovitti evolved into one of the most outstanding parodic Westerns of the genre*

Gai Luron, not quite the jolly fellow his name implied, epitomized the hang-dog expression in his morose commentary on life

In a gentler vein, Marcel Gotlib created *Gai Luron* for the comic magazine **Vaillant** in 1962. Appearing at first under the title *Nanar et Jujube*, *Gai Luron* evolved as a morose and sarcastic canine philosopher whose world-weary comments on the indignities of life proved endearingly popular to French audiences.

In 1963 another landmark in French comics appeared on the scene: *Fort Navajo*, created by the

Jean Giraud, master of the action-packed adventure strip, creates train mayhem in his famous Lieutenant Blueberry *strip which originated in 1963*

Greg's Achille Talon *provided French readers with a brilliant satire on middle-class philistinism*

writer Charlier and artist Jean Giraud ('Gir') was published in **Pilote**. The story was transformed into the highly successful *Lieutenant Blueberry* series the following year. Hailed as one of the most superlative Western strips to come out of Europe, *Lieutenant Blueberry* owed much of its success to its inspired artwork and masterful action sequences. Jean Giraud, under his other pseudonym 'Moebius', went on to become the most influential French-language comics artist of the last thirty years.

On the humour side, 1963 also saw the creation of *Achille Talon* by Greg (Michel Régnier) for **Pilote**. A clever satire on middle-class smugness, the strip starred a middle-aged petit-bourgeois whose pomposity and boorishness knew no bounds. Bloated with his own self-import-

ance, the pot-bellied *Achille Talon* provided France with one of its funniest strips ever.

In 1964 SOCERLID (The Société Civile d'Etudes et de Recherches des Littératures Dessinées) was established in France. Founded by, among others, Pierre Couperie and Maurice Horn, SOCERLID was concerned with the Study and Research into Picture-Literature and went on to produce the specialist comics periodical **Phénix**, as well as organizing the exhibition of comic art entitled 'Bande Dessinée et Figuration Narrative' at the Palais du Louvre in 1967.

That same year saw the establishment of one of the high points of the modern European comic strip when the two-year-old French strip *Philémon* hit its stride in its third

sequence entitled *Le Naufrage du 'A'(The Stranded Man of 'A')*. Created by Othon Aristides under the pseudonym 'Fred', *Philémon* appeared in **Pilote** where the farmboy hero accidentally crossed into a parallel world. The stories were magical, imaginative and surreal, in many ways being somewhat reminiscent of *Krazy Kat* in its inventiveness and unpredictability.

It must be noted at this point that comics in Europe from the 1960s onward were profoundly influenced by films, and vice-versa. For example, French cinema inspired strips, styles and atmospheres that appeared in comics. Film stars were often used as models for comic characters. In reverse, film directors frequently took inspiration from the comic pages and the two media became interlinked.

The surreal landscapes of Fred's
Philémon *adorn one of the comic
world's most inspired creations of
recent times*

*Diabolik one of the first 'negative'
heroes of Italian comics, inspired a
new wave of 'fumetti neri' to flood
the Italian market*

A number of comic artists crossed the line to work on film sets and special effects. Many directors, too, were eager to make films of the strips they admired. Italy's Federico Fellini, for example, had the notion of making a film of the American *Mandrake the Magician* strip, an ambition that would have been a delight if it had been realized.

Following the student uprising in France in 1968, the French intellectual Left took up the US Underground comics and BDs became known in France as *The Ninth Art*. Adult comics had truly arrived.

Italy was also extremely active in the comics field throughout the 1960s. As well as hosting the first European Comics Congress at Bordighera in 1965 and the second at Lucca in 1966 (where it has now become a distinguished regular event), the Italians produced a mass of original and ground-breaking material. In 1962, A. & L. Guissani created *Diabolik*, a strip with a superheroic anti-hero which ushered in the era of the *fumetti neri* (black comics). Due to their violence and supposed immorality, these were for adults only.

In 1964, the first Italian comic book to feature an anti-hero as protagonist appeared – entitled **Kriminal**. Created by 'Magnus and Bunker' (Luciano Secchi and Roberto Raviola), **Kriminal**, with its strong elements of sex and sadism, caused an outcry which led to law-suits, seizures and the eventual transformation of the eponymous anti-hero into a suave gentleman burglar instead of a cold-blooded killer.

*Kriminal soon became one of the
most popular comic heroes in
Italy, despite his cruelty and
wickedness, after he first appeared
in 1964*

109

Far from being of the same calibre as Diabolik *and* Kriminal, *strips such as* Isabella *were more vulgar than creative*

A German translation of Italian master Guido Crepax's Valentina *in which fantasy almost supersedes reality*

By this time the sex-violence comic books had attracted numerous other Italian publishers to the field. **Satanik, Sadik, Goldrake, Zakimort, Isabella, Jungla, Justine, Jessica, Jacula** and **Uranella** were just a few of the titles to emerge. Many of these were vulgar and shoddily drawn; all contained cruelty and sadistic violence as routine occurrences. Every form of sexual depravity was utilized, with bestiality, flagellation and fetishism taking pride of place.

It was not surprising that several of these comics were taken to court in 1966 'for instigating crime and violating general moral feelings'. The charges were dismissed, however, on the grounds of Italy's legally guaranteed press freedom.

Not all of the *fumetti neri* were devoid of artistic merit and originality. **Diabolik** and **Kriminal** were innovative and worthy contributions to the Italian comics field. Along with so many other Italian efforts of the Sixties, they contributed to the prevailing quality of the genre and prompted not only the comics conventions in Italy but the establishment of the excellent comic monthly **Linus** in 1965.

One of the first contributors to **Linus** was Guido Crepax, an innovative

master of the comic idiom who helped revolutionize the comic form, both in content and structure. His creation of *Neutron* for **Linus** in 1965 eventually evolved into the world-renowned strip *Valentina*, a sexual journey through the heroine's fantasies and hallucinations and one of the most significant European strips of the last twenty-five years.

Crepax has become one of the best-known Italian comic artists with his creation of further notable strips

Hugo Pratt's offbeat Sgt. Kirk *was one of the best of the Western strips to emerge from Argentina during Pratt's fifteen-year stint in South America*

Corto Maltese, *created by Italian Hugo Pratt in 1970, became one of the most popular French-language strips when it appeared first in France and then in Belgium*

including *L'Astronave Pirata, La Casa Matta, Alexandre Newski, Belinda, Bianca* and *Histoire d'O*. He is also a very successful book illustrator and animator. Known by some as 'the Raphael of the comics'. Crepax remains both controversial and fascinating.

On a less esoteric note, Italy's other most celebrated comic artist, Hugo Pratt, returned home in 1965 after working in South America and England from 1950. While in South America he had created *Sgt Kirk* (1953), *Ernie Pike* (1956), *Anna della Jungla* (1959) and *Wheeling*, among a host of other strips. Many of these were obviously reminiscent of Milton Caniff's art, but upon his return to Italy, Hugo Pratt established his own striking style which determined his place as the 'Godfather of *fumetti*' – and as one of the most popular and best-known European cartoonists.

Pratt worked at first for **Corriere dei Piccolo** in Milan before moving on in 1967 to the monthly **Sgt Kirk**. For the next three years he contributed the title strip, a cavalry Western that found instant popularity with readers, as well as *Capitan Cormorand, Luck Star O'Hara* and, most notably, *Una Ballata del Mare Salato*. The latter strip provided the character who went on to star in Pratt's pièce de résistance *Corto Maltese*, created for the French comic **Pif** in 1970.

Corto Maltese was an adventure strip of the highest order, combining historical adventures of the eponymous sea captain with magic and witchcraft to create an atmosphere heavy in sound and fury and surrealism. Pratt transferred his strip from **Pif** to the Belgian **Tintin** in 1974 where it went on to gain even wider popularity, all the episodes being reprinted in book form and translated into many languages.

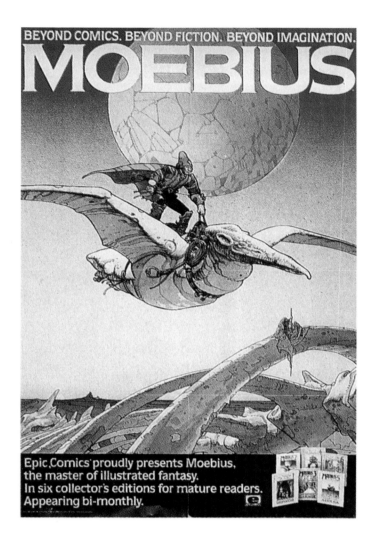

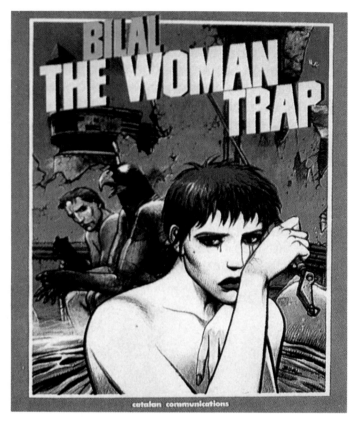

Enki Bilal's brooding cover for **The Woman Trap**, *the sequel to his legendary* **Gods in Chaos** *album*

Epic Comics produced this poster to publicize translations of Moebius's masterpiece Arzach and Other Fantasies

Strictly for adults

The 1970s and 1980s saw the mutation of European comics into elegant and sophisticated hard-cover strip albums and magazines for adult readership. The graphic novel was pioneered in Europe, notably by the three most progressive comics-producing nations: France, Italy and Spain.

An explosion of adults-only BD magazines in France brought renown to one particularly inspired artist — Jean Giraud. Following his success with *Lieutenant Blueberry* in the 1960s under the pseudonym 'Gir', Giraud now began work in the science fiction field under the name Moebius. In the mid-1970s he helped to found the radical new adult magazine **Métal Hurlant** for which he wrote and drew some of his finest work.

The translated **Heavy Metal** gave American and English readers the chance to enjoy the mastery of one of Europe's finest comic artists; and in 1987 Marvel Comics' Epic line undertook to publish a series of trade paperback albums entitled **Moebius — The Collected Fantasies of Jean Giraud**, which received a great deal of praise when published in the United States.

Giraud later settled in California, renouncing themes of sex or violence in order to work on American comics, including superhero sagas. But his adult masterpieces of the Seventies and Eighties, including the strange and silent **Arzach**, the improvisational **Airtight Garage**, the six-part **Incal** series and his Zen-influenced **The Gardens of Aedena**, testify to the undeniable genius which has made Moebius the most powerful influence on Euro-comics in recent years.

Another influential science-fantasy comic artist to have achieved a resounding impact on world comics is Yugoslavian-born Enki Bilal, whose Lovecraftian allegories and sombre fantasies appeared in French BDs from the 1970s on. In 1980 his broody and atmospheric **Gods in Chaos** album, followed by **The Woman Trap**, established him as both an artist and writer and as one of Europe's foremost science fiction cartoonists.

Although Bilal soon branched out into the film world, designing sets for Alain Resnais's *Life Is a Bed of Roses* and directing his own *Bunker Palace Hotel*, he continues to produce comic art of the highest quality in graphic novels such as **The Town That Didn't Exist** and **Exterminator**.

Francis Masse is a BD artist who made the transition from animated films to comic art in the 1970s with dense and detailed panels inspired by classical engravings. Dubbed as a 'wildly satirical Leonardo da Vinci', Masse's 1986 colour series **Les Deux du Balcon** bridged the worlds of nonsense and science with a talented ease and precision.

One of the first BD artists to break from the conventional 48-pages-in-colour album format was the renowned writer and illustrator, Jacques Tardi, who preferred working in black-and-white and felt that the stories should be as long as necessary. In the French magazine **À Suivre**, established in 1978, he created true novels (*BD Romans*) which paved the way for a new maturity in French comics.

Tardi's most popular commercial series was a parody melodrama set in belle-époque Paris and entitled **The Extraordinary Adventures of Adèle Blanc Sec**, contained in six full-colour albums.

On a far more severe note, his ongoing series **War of the Trenches** reveals his deep and obsessional anti-war feelings. This bleakly realistic depiction of incidents from the First World War stems from his grandfather's wartime experiences and from his father's six-year internment in a prison camp during the Second World War.

Tardi's recent work also includes adaptations of two Leo Malet detective novels, the surrealistic epic **Ici Même**, the Felliniesque **Polonius** and **Tueur de Cafards** (Cockroach

The above pages from Francis Masse's Les Deux du Balcon *demonstates aptly his originality and talent. The lower panel depicts a museum display showing Mickey Mouse's evolutionary development*

Jacques Tardi's Adèle Blanc-Sec, *purportedly based on the life of writer George Sand, offers an unparalleled occult history of the Belle Epoque. The first volume appeared in 1976, entitled* **Adèle et la Bête**

*Scenes fom Jacques Tardi's bleak depiction of
World War I,* War of the Trenches, *an ongoing
series since 1983*

Javier Mariscal's delightfully fresh and colourful Los
Garriris *demonstrates his distinctive style and humour*

Black humour from Italy in the form of Mattioli's Squeak the Mouse, *a brash
and brightly coloured gore-toon where the antics of mouse and tom-cat carry
the* Tom and Jerry *theme way too far*

Lorenzo Mattotti's Fires *as
presented in 1988 by Catalan
Communications for English and
American consumption*

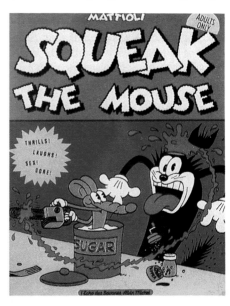

Killer), all of the latter being collaborations with other writers.

One cannot leave the French contributions to comics without mentioning one of the country's modern masters of mood: Jacques de Loustal. Utilizing warm and evocative watercolours, de Loustal produced **Hearts of Sand** and **Barney and the Blue Note**. His collaboration with writer Philippe Paringaux on **Love Shots** prompted reviewers to refer to the duo as a blend of Hockney and Hemingway.

Spain was a late developer in the field of comics due to Franco's stifling state censorship. Publishers of adult comics were threatened with imprisonment under Franco's regime and it was not until after his death in 1975 that a wealth of new magazines emerged. The no-holds-barred **El Vibora** (The Viper) became the vehicle for Spain's eternally optimistic Javier Mariscal whose warmth and exuberance are aptly displayed in his *Los Garriris*, the colourful adventures of Fermin and Piker. Mariscal's work also appeared in Art Spiegelman's American publication, **Raw**, as well as the book **Read Yourself Raw**.

In Italy the adult comics of the Seventies and Eighties were alive and thriving with *fumetti* artists such as Massimo Mattioli founding **Il Male**, **Cannibale** and the notorious **Frigidaire**. Mattioli's contributions included the strips *Superwest*, *Joe Galaxy* (sex and science fiction) and *Squeak the Mouse*, a surreal, silent and gory strip about a promiscuous tomcat being terrorized by a killer-zombie mouse.

In 1980 Lorenzo Mattotti formed the experimental Valvoline group in Italy. Mattotti's masterpiece **Fires** is considered one of the most striking and original works ever done in the medium.

In Holland Joost Swarte combined underground sensibilities with Hergé's classicism while Belgium's graphic stylist Ever Meulen was one of a number of artists who emerged in response to underground propaganda. All over Europe a new sophistication and style characterized the adult comics which prevailed as a new art form risen from the world's hotbed of culture.

A richly coloured scene from Jacques de Loustal's Love Shots *(1985), American vignettes of sun, the 'good life' and fading starlets*

It is impossible to mention every important contributor to adult Euro-comics. Suffice to say, these comics and their associated graphic novels and albums have heralded a revolution in comic style the world over.

During the last two decades European comics for children have been a mixture of indigenous strips and imports that have tended to swamp them. All European countries have benefited from an interchange of comics and strips from one another and from the rest of the world. In Portugal, for example, children read comics from Spain, Brazil and Argentina. International distributors such as Editora Globo in Brazil provide *piccolo* format comics such as **Chico Bento** and **A turma do Arrepio Roonc!** for the Portuguese news-stands. These contain South American strips interspersed with occasional American characters like *Beetle Bailey* .

Yet another example of cross-fertilization is Portugal's **Jornal da B.D.** containing reprints of some of the best European strips including *Asterix, Achille Talon, Lucky Luke* and *Lieutenant Blueberry.*

Spain, for its part, has succeeded in producing a number of original comics for children containing lively indigenous strips by artists such as 'Jan', Vasquez, Segura, Escobar and Gosse. Titles include **Zipizape, Pulgarcito, Super Lopez** and **Mortadelo.** 1980s reprints of earlier successes, such as **El Guerrero del Antifaz** (created in 1944) vie with reprints of **Popeye** and **Flash Gordon** on an equal footing.

So whereas the Europeans continue to produce their own brand of comics, they have access to strips from all over the world. Their own comics are exported to the USA, Japan and South America in increasing quantities, and appear prominently as major participants in a truly international comics scene.

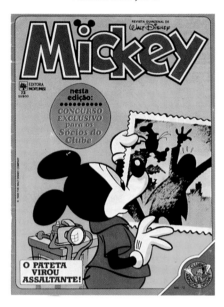

The ever-popular adventures of Mickey Mouse and the Disney stable of characters are presented in Editora Morumbi's **Mickey** *comic for Portugal's numerous fans*

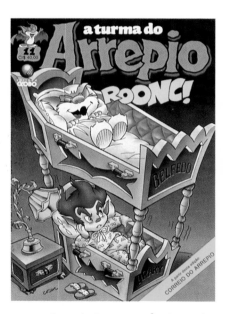

Cesar's **A turma do Arrepio** *resembles a cross between Disney characters and the Smurfs in this small but colourful Editora Globo offering*

Mauricio's cover for the popular **Chico Bento** *comic, appearing in Portugal courtesy of Editora Globo*

The cover of Portugal's **Jornal da B.D.** *features the popular French character,* Achille Talon, *with reprints inside*

Full colour original humour strips adorn Spain's **Super Lopez**, *No. 1, which appeared in 1987*

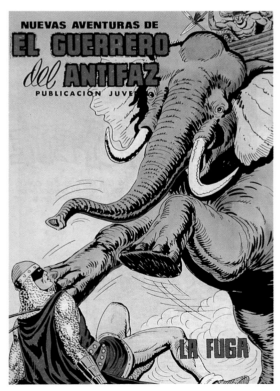

It looks like curtains for El Guerrero del Antifaz *in this Spanish reprint, but our hero survives the arrows in his back and the might of the elephant to defeat his enemies*

From the same stable as **Super Lopez**, **Zipizape** *was produced and printed in Spain by Ediciones B*

SHOTARO ISHINOMORI

JAPAN

WITH AN INTRODU

Unemployment should go down! We need more jobs before the election!

Restrict

NOV. 1955 (G) TENSE, EXCITING ACTION! FIRST ISSUE 9ᴰ

ANTI CRIME SQUAD

FP

MANDRAKE
The Magician
Nᵒ 2

EVERY PAGE IN COLO

Captain

TRIUMPH

Nᵒ 10 6ᴰ

I HATE

AARDVARK-VANAHEIM PRESENTS

CEREBUS
THE AARDVARK

COMICS
AROUND THE WORLD

Outside the United States and Europe most countries are highly reliant on imports and translations from these two principal comics-producing areas. But among the nations which have had a considerable influence on the genre with their own indigenous publications, particular mention should be made of Canada, Japan, Australia and New Zealand, China, Russia, Scandinavia, Argentina and the Philippines.

In Canada the comics industry suffered a number of ups and downs, but several worthwhile features evolved despite the competition from over the border. The first English-Canadian comic art appeared in the early 1900s as an outgrowth of political cartoons such as those that had appeared in John Henry Walker's **Punch in Canada** (which made its début in 1849 and was modelled on its English namesake), **The Jester**, **The Grumbler** and **Grinchuckle**, all successful satirical journals of the nineteenth century.

Canada's most important cartoonist before the turn of the century was John Wilson Bengough who in 1893 launched a cartoon weekly entitled **Grip** which lasted for twenty-one years. Another accomplished artist of the period was Henri Julien who became the country's first full-time news cartoonist when he joined the Montreal **Star** in 1888.

Strips soon began appearing in Canadian newspapers, such as *Pierre et Pierette* by Russell Patterson in **La Patrie** and Arch Dale's *The Doo-Dads* which was syndicated throughout North America. In 1921 Jimmy Frise created the strip *Life's Little Comedies* for the Toronto **Star Weekly**. It was later retitled *Birdseye Centre* and it became the longest-running Canadian comic strip, continuing to run until Frise's death in 1948 (having transferred to the Montreal **Standard** in 1947 under the title *Juniper Junction*). With its

gentle touch of slapstick humour and satire, *Birdseye Centre* represented everyone's dream of small town life and became a Canadian institution.

One of Canada's most famous comic sons, Hal Foster of *Prince Valiant* fame, had his *Tarzan* strip appearing in Canada from 1929 – although it was published in the United States. This was to prove a recurring problem for Canadian comics as most of their best artists and writers ended up with American firms instead of Canadian publishers.

In 1933 Canada's first indigenous adventure strip appeared under the title *Men of the Mounted*, soon to be followed by *Robin Hood & Co*, both written by Ted McCall.

With the arrival of the American superhero comics in the late 1930s, the popularity of the medium increased throughout Canada. However, war economy import restrictions in 1940 soon stemmed the flow from over the border. This

Anglo-American's **Freelance Comic** *(1941 to 1946) offered action and thrills set in the Canadian wilderness with stories by Ted McCall and art by Ed Furness*

A montage of Anglo-American's
leading characters from the
late 1940s

Century Publications produced **Bombadier Comics** *in
the mid-1940s. Stories ranged from science-fiction to
swashbuckling to Western strips. Oddly enough, the
characters portrayed on the colourful cover bore no
relation to the stories within*

enabled Canada's home-grown industry to flourish.

By 1941 English-Canadian black-and-white comics had begun to appear on the news-stands, spear-headed by the country's first true Canadian comic book with original strips, **Better Comics**, published by Maple Leaf Publishing and followed a month later by Anglo-American's **Robin Hood and Company Comic**, containing reprints.

Other Canadian publishers soon joined the fray, including Hill-borough Studios (**Triumph Adventure Comics**, 1941), Commercial Signs of Canada (**Wow Comics**, 1941), Educational Projects of

Montreal (**Canadian Heroes**, 1942) and Feature Publications of Toronto (**Lightning Comics**, 1944). In the meantime, Maple Leaf had expanded its line to include **Bing Bang Comics, Lucky Comics**, and **Rocket Comics**, while Anglo-American had added **Freelance, Grand Slam** and **Three Aces**.

Commercial Signs, run by Cyril Bell, absorbed Hillborough Studios in 1942 and became Bell Features, Canada's best-known comic pub-lisher, under art director Adrian Dingle. Dingle had created what was to become one of Canada's most memorable characters, *Nel-vana of the Northern Lights* for **Tri-umph Adventure** in 1941 and he

brought his comic and his super-heroine with him when he joined Bell. He also created a crime-fight-ing strip entitled *The Penguin*, as well as *The Sign of Freedom* and *Nils Grant, Private Investigator*, and he contributed colour cover art for many of Bell's titles including **Dime, Active, Joke, Commando** and **Dizzy Don**, in addition to **Triumph**.

Unfortunately this burst of creative enthusiasm among Canadian pub-lishers, artists and writers was cut short at the end of the war when US comics reappeared on news-stands in Canada. Although they tried to change to full colour printing, the competiton was too great and most original titles ceased to exist.

In order to stay afloat, publishers such as Anglo-American and newcomer Superior Publishers printed Canadian editions of American comics, but by the early 1950s, after Canada's Fulton Bill (1949) and America's creation of the Comics Code Authority (1954) had brought censorship of comics into force, even the reprint industry ground to a halt.

In the Sixties and Seventies most indigenous Canadian comics were educational or advertising give-aways published by Comic Book World and other companies. However, the birth of underground comics in the United States in the late Sixties brought about a new wave in Canada which started slowly but gained momentum in the Seventies and Eighties.

The first Canadian new-wave literary comic to appear was **Scraptures** in 1967, followed by **Operation Missile** in 1968. In 1969 Canada had its first underground comic, **Snore Comix**, leading the way for a three-year flurry of activity which saw the titles **Flash Theatre**, **Hierographics**, **Polar Funnies**, **White Lunch** and others exploring sex, drugs, radical politics and rock.

In the mid-1970s the focus shifted to more traditional adult-oriented science fiction and fantasy themes with publications such as **Andromeda, Out of the Depths, Orb, Arik Khan, Phanacea, Fog City** and **Cerebus the Aardvark** leading the way. **Cerebus the Aardvark**, created by Dave Sim, began as a sword and sorcery parody in 1977 and evolved into a sophisticated publication which became Canada's longest-running comic book. This period also brought a boom in fan organizations and magazines across the country. In 1975 the first International Festival of Comics was held at the University of Montreal.

In 1979, after his introduction in

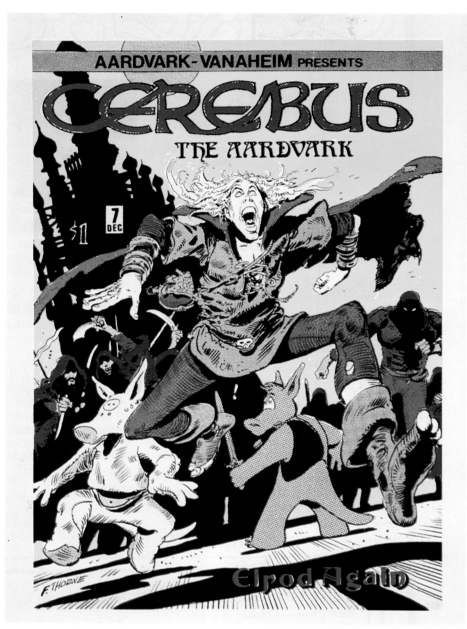

Making its début in December 1977, **Cerebus the Aardvark** *has become the longest-running Canadian comic book and perhaps the country's greatest comic achievement*

1975, **Captain Canuck,** a Canadian superhero comic of the highest order, returned as a slick alternative comic. Once again, if only for fourteen issues, Canada had its own superhero.

Throughout the 1980s, Canada played a key role in the development of the alternative publishing industry. In 1984 there were more than a dozen titles being distributed throughout North America. **Neil the Horse Comics and Stories, Journey, Quadrant, Yummy Fur, Casual Casual Comics, No Name Comix** and **Cerebus Jam** were a few of the Canadian titles to achieve success.

In French-speaking Canada the Quebec BDs (*Bandes Dessinées*) rarely survived for even two years, although the first French-Canadian newspaper strip had appeared as long ago as 1904 when *Le Père Ladebauche* by J. Charlebois was published in **La Presse**. With a wealth of American imports as well as European titles to choose from,

Heralding the Silver Age of Canadian comics, Richard Comely's **Captain Canuck** *No. 1 of July 1975 is now a prime collectors' item*

A page from the Cerebus the Aardvark *strip demonstrates the originality of this sword and sorcery parody*

the main indigenous magazines of note were **Ma(r)de In Kebec, BD, L'Ecran, Les Aventures du Capitaine Kebec, Prisme, L'Illustré** and **Baloune** in the 1970s. Their most long-lived product, **Croc,** began publication in 1979 and became the only Quebec mass-market magazine to publish comic art regularly throughout the 1980s.

The Hokusai tradition

Japan is the one of the few non-Western countries to have established its own comics tradition. Approximately one-third of all books and magazines sold over the course of a year are comic books. The comic format is used to educate as well as amuse, as in Shotaro Ishinomori's 310-page introduction to Japanese economics entitled **Japan, Inc.**

The definitive monograph about Japanese comic books, **Manga! Manga!** (1986) by F.L. Schodt, gives the full story, but a book on world comics would be incomplete without at least a brief history of the more important landmarks of Japanese comics.

Japan's comic history goes back as far as 1814 when the **Hokusai Manga** (*The Hokusai Cartoons*, the first of fifteen volumes) was published. The artist Hokusai is credited with bringing the tradition of the European cartoon to Japan, thus paving the way for the introduction of Western-style comic books in later years.

In 1905 Rakuten Kitazawa founded the first Japanese cartoon magazine, **Tokyo Puck**, which was modelled on the American **Puck**.

His creations of *Doncia* and *Tonda Haneko* reflected the techniques and ideas inherent in the work of American cartoonists but showed an originality that was to keep Japan on a level with American innovations. It was Kitazawa who generalized the word *manga* to encompass both cartoon and comic strips and who is credited with establishing the modern comic strip in Japan. Omiya's City Museum of Cartoon Art, established in 1966, is dedicated to him.

Japan, like the rest of the world, received an influx of the top-notch American strips. *Mutt and Jeff*

By the mid-1980s the benkyo manga (study comics) had become established in Japan. Quick and handy ways to learn about useful subjects, these comics took on a new sophistication with the arrival of full-length books in comic strip format like **Japan, Inc.** *which was published in 1986 by the Japanese equivalent of the* **Wall Street Journal** *and became an instant best-seller*

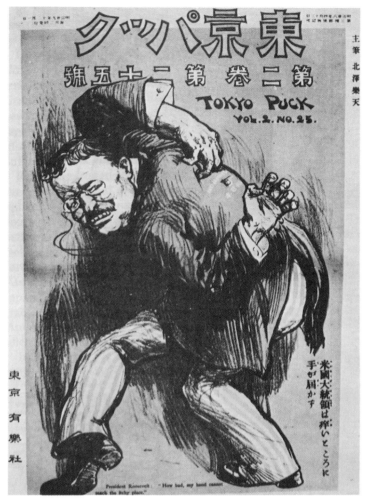

This 1906 issue of **Tokyo Puck** *showing Teddy Roosevelt trying to reach an 'anti-Japanese' wasp reflects the concern of the Japanese with regard to the discriminatory laws being passed against them in the US.* **Tokyo Puck** *was the most international magazine to have been produced in Japan*

Rakuten Kitazawa provided Japan's first serialized comic strip in 1902 with Tagosaku to Mokube no Tokyo Kembutsu *(Tagosaku and Mokube sightseeing in Tokyo)*

Japan's answer to America's Bringing Up Father *was Yutaka Aso's* Nonki na Tosan *(Easy-going Daddy) which first appeared in 1924*

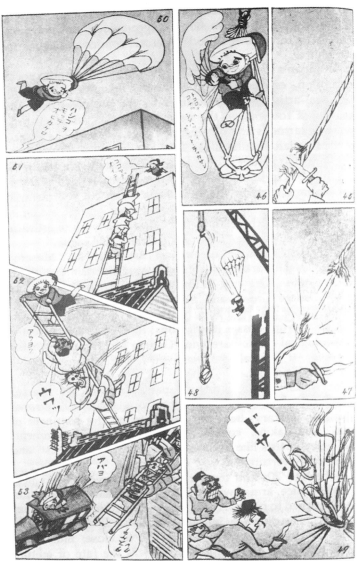

Sako Shishido's Spido Taro *first appeared in the* **Yomiuri Sunday Manga** *in 1930 and immediately captivated its readers with its American-style cliff-hanging action and panel layouts*

Sazae-San *by Machiko Hasegawa was Japan's first family strip when it made its début in the* **Asahi** *newspaper in 1946. After a run of almost 30 years, it was serialized in 68 volumes of cartoon books which remain popular today*

reprints, for example, appeared from 1910 onwards. The first original daily newspaper strip to appear in Japan was Yutako Aso's *Nonki na Tosan* (Easy-going Daddy) in **Hochi** in 1924. Created to bolster the spirits of people whose homes were destroyed by the earthquake in 1923, *Nonki na Tosan* proved a resounding success and ran in various Japanese papers until 1950.

Yutako Aso became one of Japan's most prolific artists throughout the 1920s and into the 1930s. He excelled at responding to his

public's moods with topical strips and in 1933, when the Great Depression was at its peak in Japan, Aso created *Todano Bonji* (Average Boy) concerning the unemployment which was causing a social problem at the time.

In 1930 the **Yomiuri Sunday Manga** carried a strip by Sako Shishido entitled *Spido Taro (Speedy)* which was to revolutionize the Japanese

comics. Having studied in the United States, Shishido introduced American techniques well removed from the prevalent Japanese convention of traditional plots and portrayals. By utilizing framing, space manipulation and other devices, the artist achieved a new look for Japanese comic strips.

Japan's most famous pre-war comic strip was Suiho Tagawa's *Norakuro*

Suiho Tagawa's Norakuro (Black Stray) *concerned a bumbling dog who led his army into battle from 1931 to 1941 in the* **Shonen Club** *comic. But the dog lieutenant eventually got the thumbs down from the Japanese Imperial Army who deemed the strip bad for their image*

which first appeared in the monthly **Shonen Kurabu** in 1931. *Norakuro* was a stray dog who joined the 'fierce dog regiment' and eventually became a professional soldier-dog.

The development of the strip over the years reflected the militarism that was prevalent in Japan during the war years, and although it ceased to be published in 1941, it was revived in 1958 in the war comic **Maru** and went on to become Japan's longest-running feature.

During the early 1940s, Japanese comic production faltered and no imports were received from the US until the American occupation of Japan at the close of the war. The influx of US publications inspired a more occidental approach for Japanese comics including Japan's first family strip, *Sazae-san* (1946) by Machiko Hasegawa, as well as Soji Yamakawa's science fiction strip *Fushigina Kuni no Putcha* (1947) and his jungle adventure *Shonen Oja* (The Boy King) in 1948.

Osamu Tezuka's Tetsuwan-Atom *(Mighty Atom) was one of Japan's most internationally popular strips. Serialized in* **Shonen** *from 1952 to 1968, the strip was transformed into Japan's first animated television series in 1963. Here Atom and his surrogate father battle a dinosaur after having been transported into the past by a time machine*

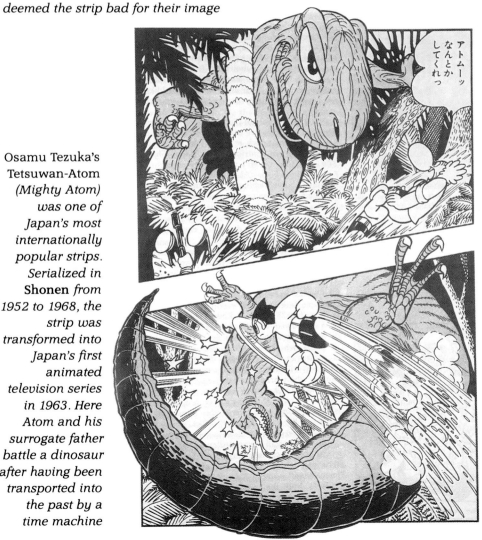

Traditionally, Japanese ninja strips are bound to shock. Here in Sanpei Shirato's Ninja Bugeicho(Chronicles of a Ninja's Military Accomplishments), Kagemuro's head is brought before the warlord Nobunaga and announces its own presence to the horror of the onlookers

For adults only, Golgo 13 first appeared in 1969 in **Big Comic**. Golgo 13, a professional assassin named Duke Togo, stalks his prey with cold-blooded nonchalance. Creator Takao Saito keeps his strip firmly outside the bounds of human morality

America's Gold Key version of Tetsuwan-Atom. This No. 1 issue appeared in August 1965

In the 1950s the comic monthly **Shonen** continued to be the show-case for some of Japan's most popular strips. In 1951 its introduction of Osamu Tezuka's science fiction strip *Tetsuwan-Atom* widened its audience yet further. *Tetsuwan- Atom*, the story of a robot endowed with human emotions, became one of the most famous and longest-running strips of post-war Japan. His phenomenal popularity led to a series of animated cartoons beginning in 1963 which were shown in over twenty countries, including the USA and UK under the title *Astroboy*.

Three other strips of particular note from the 1950s were Kon Shimizu's humorous *Kappa* strips (1951), Eiichi Fukui's *Akado Suzunosuke* (1954) and Sanpei Shirato's *Ninja Bugeicho* (1959). *Kappa no Kawataro* was the first of many sequels

about a merry band of river imps (*kappas*). The feature spawned a television series: the creations were also used in media advertisements throughout Japan in the 1960s.

After the first episode of *Akado Suzunosuke*, its creator died, leaving the story in the capable hands of artist Tsunayoshi Takeuchi until its last episode in 1960. A samurai adventure incorporating the art of fencing (kendo), the strip, like many others which achieved a high degree of popularity, inspired a series of animated cartoons.

Ninja Bugeicho appeared in comic books published exclusively for lending libraries from 1959 to 1962, during which time it inspired a host of imitations. When revived in 1966 in a mass-circulation comic book, it became an instant best-seller,

This vivid and dynamic art is from the agile pen of artist Hiroshi Hirata. Much of his work was translated into English to appear in **Manga**, *an anthology comic that brought Japan's best artists to the attention of the US and Britain*

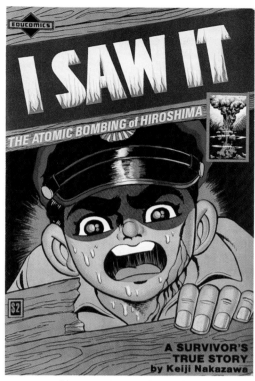

Seen first in a special issue of **Shonen Jampu** *in 1972, this vivid portrayal of the bombing of Hiroshima created quite a stir when published in the US in 1982*

elevating its creator Shirato to hero status among Japanese readers. A samurai strip set during the peasant revolts from 1560 to 1588, *Ninja Bugeicho* was famous for its gruesome scenes of death and realistic battle episodes, interspersed with romantic interludes. Shirato continued his success with a number of popular ninja strips throughout the 1960s, including, among others, *Sasuke* (1961) in **Shonen** and *Kamui Den* (1964) in **Garo**.

Osamu Tezuka followed up *Tetsuwan-Atom* with a string of successes which included horror, fantasy, Western and science fiction stories. In 1961 he founded Mushi Productions from where he produced numerous movie and television cartoons. He is the artist who is credited with bringing cinematic techniques to the Japanese comics, and his versatility and creative abilities earned him the title 'King of the Japanese Comics'.

Yet another comic artist to have had an enormous influence on contemporary Japanese comics is Takao Saito, whose work includes the detective strip *Taifu Goro* (1960) and *Gorgo 13* (1969), about a professional killer. Saito's work emphasized sex, speed and thills and gave fresh impetus to the Japanese comics field throughout the 1960s.

One of Japan's best illustrative artists during the Sixties and Seventies was Hiroshi Hirata whose realistically drawn samurai strips included *Jaken Yaburetari* (1959), *Hishu no Tachi* (1963), *Soregashi Kojikini Arazu* (1970) and *Kubidai Hikiukenin* (1973).

Another fine draftsman of the period was Koo Kojima. His elegant and erotic illustrations adorned adult strips such as *Oretacha Riva Da!* (1960), *Ahiruga Oka 77* (1961), *Nihon no Kachan* (1966) and *Oumaga Tsuji* (1971). Kojima also took

over the famous *Kappa* strip upon the death of Shimizu in 1974, transforming it from fantasy to eroticism.

There have been so many talented Japanese cartoonists over the last thirty years but special mention must go to Shunji Sonoyama for his *Gyatoruzo* (1965), Fujio Akatsuka for *Osomatsu-kun* (1962), Tatsuhiko Yamagami for *Gaki Deka* (1974), Shinji Nagashima for his autobiographical novel in comic form: the trilogy *Kiiroi Namida*, and to Keiji Nakazawa for his moving and personal portrayal of the devastation caused by the bombing of Hiroshima, *Ore wa Mita (I Saw It)* followed by his popular *Barefoot Gen* series on the same subject.

One of the most outstanding features of the last several decades in the Japanese comics field has been the development of the *animekomikkusu* (animation comics). This tradition is unique to Japan. Totally

With characters designed by Shohei Obara, The Humanoid *panels shown here derive from the latest field being explored by the Japanese comics industry.* Animekomikkusu *(animation comics) are created directly from the prints of animated films*

dependent upon visual imagery and page design, the animation comics are intended to be imitations of animation films. However, by their very nature they represent one of the purest forms of graphic communication in the world today.

The characters portrayed in *anime-komikkusu* generally have Western features and dialogue is kept to a minimum. The colours and panel layouts are all-important, as these are primarily a visual exercise to present various mythical or science fiction characters to the public. *Transformers* and *Captain Harlock and the Queen of a Thousand Days* are only two of the *animekomikkusu* successes that have derived from popular animated series.

Pop stars, jokes and humour and romance strips fill this 1986 Easter issue of a popular Japanese comic

Comics down under

While Australia's comic output never achieved the worldwide exposure of Japan's they nevertheless produced some noteworthy indigenous strips. One of the most famous of these is *The Potts* which began in 1919 as a political newspaper strip in **Smith's Weekly** entitled *You and Me*.

Originally drawn by Stan Cross, *You and Me* was Australia's first newspaper strip and concentrated mainly on topical issues. With the introduction of Mrs Pott, the strip took on a more intimate flavour, with husband and wife squabbling over various domestic issues.

In 1939 Jim Russell took over the strip and the title was changed to *Mr & Mrs Potts*. **Smith's Weekly** ceased publication in 1950 and the strip was toned down for syndication throughout Australia by the Herald and Weekly Times Ltd after changing the name to *The Potts*. The resulting feature was far more conventional for public taste and in order to make it even more of a 'family strip' new characters, such as Uncle Dick, were added over the years. By 1958 *The Potts* had achieved far-flung success and was being syndicated to thirty-five American dailies as well as to Finland, Ceylon, Turkey and several other countries.

Following hot on the heels of *The Potts*, *Ginger Meggs* (originally titled *Us Fellers*) was Australia's first full-page colour Sunday comic strip when it appeared in 1921. Drawn by Jimmy Bancks, it was also one of the few Australian strips to be syndicated overseas.

Ginge, as the lovable red-headed schoolboy hero was affectionately known, became the most popular local strip ever published in Australia. After Bancks's death in 1952, the strip was taken over by Ron Vivian who made every effort to capture its unique flair. Upon Vivian's death in 1974, *Ginger Meggs* was handled by a number of ghost artists but sank into decline.

The majority of the remaining Australian strips were created for the home market and are therefore little known abroad. *Fatty Finn*, for example, a rival of *Ginger Meggs*, had a distinctly Australian flavour from his inception in 1923 in the **Sydney Sunday News**.

Created by Syd Nicholls as a Billy Bunter-style schoolboy, *Fatty Finn* evolved over the years into a 'kid strip', which pre-empted adventure strips with tales of cannibals, pirates and highwaymen. His initial run ended in 1931 but he was revived in his own comic paper, **Fatty Finn's Weekly**, from 1934-35, then appeared in other Australian comics from 1940-45, and got his own comic back from 1946-50, entitled **Fatty Finn's Comic**. *Fatty* was taken up by newspapers again in 1951 and appeared thenceforth in the **Sunday Sun-Herald**, still drawn by Syd Nicholls.

Australia's longest-running comic strip was *Bib and Bub* by May Gibbs which ran from 1925 until 1967, ending up in the **Sunday Sun-Herald**. Essentially a fantasy strip aimed at very young children, *Bib and Bub* was based on Gibbs's delightful children's book, **Gumnut Babies** (1916).

One of Australia's most versatile and prolific comic artists, English-born Reg Hicks ('Hix'), made his mark in 1934 when he produced Australia's first worthwhile adventure strip, *Out of the Silence*. Hicks went on to contribute countless strips for the **Argus** and the **Age**, including *Robinson Crusoe* (1936), *Betty and Bob* (1936) and *The Space Patrol* (1938). He also created *The Adventures of Larry Steel* in 1937, an adventure strip which ran for three years and which was instrumental in helping to popularize the genre in Australia.

In 1941 Hicks created *Tightrope Tim* for the **Sydney Sunday Sun**, followed by his humour strip, *Family Man*, which ran in the **Sun** for twelve years. He produced four **Kid Koals** comic books in the 1950s, as well as creating *Debbie* for **The New Idea**.

During the early 1940s, one of the leading publishers of Australian comics was Frank Johnson Publications. Artists such as Cecil 'Unk' White, Rhys Williams, Carl Lyon, Emile Mercier and, perhaps most famous of all, Stanley Pitt, joined forces to produce budget publications of varying quality but with a certain amount of originality and artistic talent. Pitt went on to become one of Australia's most highly respected comic artists.

In 1946 Pitt produced the first episode of his masterful newspaper strip, *Silver Starr in the Flameworld* for the **Sunday Sun**. An avid Alex Raymond admirer, Pitt borrowed extensively from his hero's style and the resulting panels were some of the most beautifully rendered comic art to be produced in Australia.

In 1948 Pitt created *Captain Power* for the **Sunday Herald** but he left the paper in 1949 after a salary dispute. Collaborating with his brother Reginald, Paul Wheelahan and Frank and Jimmy Ashley, the team produced 32 issues of **Yarmak Comics** for Young's Merchandising. These, together with **Silver Starr Super Comics**, were bound together for reprint albums such as 'The Giant Comic Annual'.

Another exponent of the adventure strip in Australia was Syd Miller whose *Rod Craig* ran from 1946–55. This strip was also syndicated in Paris, Buenos Aires and Jamaica

Stanley Pitt's homage to Flash Gordon, Silver Starr *battled relentlessly against evil-doers on alien worlds.* Six Silver Starr Super Comics *were published by Youngs Merchandising Co. in the early 1950s*

Stanley Pitt's title page from Silver Starr Super Comic *No. 3 which contained reprints of the 1940s' newspaper strip*

Issue No. 1 of Stanley Pitt's famed Silver Starr Super Comic *shows the eponymous hero rescuing the voluptuous maiden Pristine with verve and valour*

The Yarmak Jungle King Comic, *created by Stanley Pitt in 1949, ran for 32 issues. The Lord of the Belgian Congo bore more than a passing resemblance to Tarzan* and it set a precedent in its own country for competing successfully with imported adventure strips. As in most countries worldwide, American imports stifled local efforts, with few exceptions. *Rod Craig* was one such exception and was even adapted for radio.

Two other strips which originated in the 1940s and were extremely popular were Alex Gurney's *Bluey and Curley* (1940), a nationalistic hum-our strip about army life, and Stan Cross's *Wally and the Major* (1940), on the same army theme but per-haps not so blatantly Australian. Both proved to be long-running sur-vivors with continued popularity.

The 1950s saw an increase in imported American comics reach-ing Australia. Among the most pop-ular were *Batman* and *Superman* reprints with glorious colour covers and black-and-white stories.

Produced by K.G. Murray Publish-ers of Sydney, the titles included **Batman Super Comics**, and **Super-Adventure Comic**. All of these con-tained filler humour and adventure strips – some reprints and some Australia's own.

Captain Triumph Comic, also pro-duced by K.G. Murray, was in full colour and contained Australian features including *Captain Triumph* (Lance Gallant touches the birth-

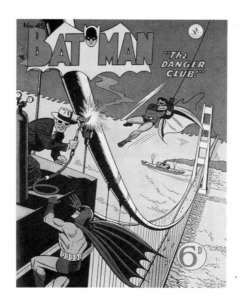

The artwork on **Captain Triumph Comics** *was less than masterful but K.G. Murray Publishers managed to gain some readers with full colour on every page*

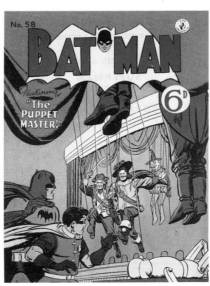

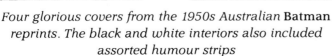
Four glorious covers from the 1950s Australian **Batman** *reprints. The black and white interiors also included assorted humour strips*

The action-packed **Anti-Crime Squad** *comic from*
November 1955 appeared monthly until the influx
of American reprints halted its progress

mark on his wrist to merge with the all-seeing spirit of his dead twin brother!), *Floogy the Figi*, *Beezy* and *Molly the Model*.

Other Australian publishers also attempted to break the American stranglehold with black-and-white adventure comics like **Anti-Crime Squad** (Gordon & Gotch Publications, 1955) and the more accomplished **True Pirate Comics** (a Frank Johnson Publication), but their efforts were short-lived. With the introduction of yet more American comics in the late 1950s the Australian comics' fate was sealed. American jungle tales were particularly popular with **Ka'a'nga Jungle King**, **Jungle Comics** and **Sheena, Queen of the Jungle** all proving very successful.

Australian newspaper strips nevertheless continued to flourish with new examples being added from time to time. One of the more successful was *Air Hawk and the Flying Doctors*, an adventure strip created by former comic artist John Dixon. Appearing first in the Sydney **Sunday Herald** in 1959, *Air Hawk* was popular enough to become a daily strip as well in 1963. In 1970, Hart Amos took over the Sunday strip which continued to flourish under his sure hand. Dixon continued with the daily strip, portraying the outback adventures of the flying doctor, *Jim Hawk*, with verve and vitality.

New Zealand, like Australia, had a deluge of reprint issues including **Feature Comics** (Walt Disney

Another 1950s Frank Johnson publication, **True Pirate Comics** *featured the formidable* Mrs Ching *among others, with art by Phil Belbin, Ian Alison and Peter Chapman*

New Zealand reprints of the Brick Bradford *newspaper strip, drawn by Clarence Gray, were published by Feature Productions in the 1950s*

Mandrake and Lothar go in search of the lovely Narda in this New Zealand reprint of the 1945 King Features newspaper strip

In the late 1940s **Big-Time Comics** *combined indigenous New Zealand adventures with British humour strips like* Nelson Twigg, The Boy Tec *by Roy Wilson*

reprints), **Brick Bradford** and **Mandrake the Magician** with colour covers and black-and-white or single-colour interiors.

Published in the 1950s, titles such as **Big-Time Comics** contained reprints from various British comics as well as occasional indigenous strips. Other quite crude offerings, but with occasional glimmers of charm, included **Secret Service K-7, The Blue Ghost, Supreme Feature Comics, I Hate Crime** and, worst of all, **The Adventures of Captain Havoc and the Phantom Knight** and **Real Life Adventure**.

Times Printing Works of Auckland produced a number of crime-fighting publications including this issue of I Hate Crime *from the early 1950s*

Another Times Printing Works Publication, **Invisible Avenger Comics** *featured* The Blue Ghost *and other secret agent strips*

Change in China

China was one of the only countries not to have been overwhelmed by American imports. Their indigenous comics have been totally true to their culture since their origins. Mythological and everyday scenes were painted on silk and walls as early as the third century BC and illustrated novels began appearing during the thirteenth and fourteenth centuries.

By the late 1800s, small picture-story books based on classical novels and dramas had become exceedingly popular in the large cities and fine artists began to be attracted to this accessible form of graphic communication.

After the cultural enlightment movement in the 1920s, picture-story books began to be mass produced throughout China. Until this time comic artists had been somewhat downgraded, but in the early 1930s, the great Chinese writer Lu Xun called upon writers and artists

to become more involved in the picture-story form in an article entitled 'In Defence of Comics'. Both he and his contemporary, Mao Dun, are responsible for popularizing the comics in China and for presenting them as a totally acceptable form of mass education.

Chinese picture-story books begin with a script, usually based on popular historical stories, operas or dramas. They are based not only on Chinese literature but also on Western works such as those by William Shakespeare, Victor Hugo and Mark Twain, and they present high ethical and moral standards for children and adults to emulate. Artists are then commissioned to illustrate the scripts, usually in a realistic style using line drawings, woodcuts, ink and wash, watercolour, oils or paper cuts.

The Red Detachment of Women, perhaps China's most famous comic book, was first published in 1966. The story was adapted by scriptwriter Sung Yu-chieh from the

well-known fictional work by the great Chinese author, Liang Hsin. Set in 1930 on the island of Hainan, **The Red Detachment** was representative of the 'socialist realism' then prevalent in China: an escaped slave-woman forms a Red Army detachment of women to fight landowners, capitalists and other class enemies in an adventure tale of considerable suspense and intrigue. The artwork by Lin Tzu-shun combined traditional Chinese design with Western composition, and the resulting comic was phenomenally successful in China and Hong Kong.

In 1983 China established its Chinese Comic Art Research Society to promote the theoretical study and creation of comics. Then in 1985 the Chinese Comics Publishing House was founded. Picture-stories, a term which encompasses newspaper strips, comic books and adult drama stories, are now the most popular reading material in China. Collecting and exchanging them is a favourite pastime among both children and adults.

The comics have been supported by the government as having great educational value, competitions and exhibitions have been organized and the number of comic artists

A magnificent colour plate from Yu Dawu's Cheng Tang and Xia Jie, *the story of how Cheng Tang won the people's support and ruled an empire*

has increased greatly. In recent years, there have been approximately 700 million Chinese picture-story books published.

Now, in an effort to promote international friendship and understanding, Chinese comics have come out of the closet and are exhibited worldwide at comic art conventions and festivals. Artists such as Wang Huaiqi (**Keep the Red Flag**

Flying), Chen Guoqiang (**Lives of the Scholars, The Man Who Took It With Him** and **A Wooden Man with a Stone Heart**), He Youzhi (**The White Glow**), Gao Yun (**Palace of Longevity** and **Lo Lun Takes an Examination**), Zhao Qi Xu Yong Gu Liantan (**Gada Miren, Before Starting Off** and **Singer of the People**) and Yu Dawu (**Cheng Tang and Xia Jie**) have become known and appreciated in many countries.

《成汤和夏桀》   作者：于大武

Gao Yun's Palace of Longevity *won first prize at the Jiangsu Comics Exhibition. Taken from an opera, the story is both a tale of love and a critique of the ruling classes' decadence*

Yugoslavia's Herlock Sholmes *and* Doctor Waston *appear in this humorous adaptation of Conan Doyle's detective stories*

Finnish artist Tove Jansson adapted her children's book creations into a daily newspaper strip Moomin *for the* **London Evening News** *(1954–68)*

Linking East and West

Russia and the Eastern European bloc of countries also had a tradition of cartoon and comic art. In pre-revolutionary Russia, there were a number of illustrated satire sheets published including **Budilnik** in Moscow and **Strezoka** in St Petersburg. Poland had turn-of-the-century cartoons published in the magazines **Mucha** (Flea) and **Djabel** (Devil), and in 1932 the popular *Fiki-Miki* strip was created by Makusynski and Walentinowitz.

Yugoslavia produced *Stari Macak* by Andrija Maurovic in 1937 and, more recently, *Herlock Sholmes* scored a big hit in the 1960s. Created in 1957 by Jules Radilovic and Zvonimir Furtinger, *Herlock Sholmes* made his début in 1967 in the comic weekly **Plavi Vjesnik**. In this fanciful adaptation of 'Sherlock Holmes', its two creators displayed humour, imagination and a delightful sense of the absurd.

With the erosion of barriers between East and West in the late 1980s,

it is now safe to presume that former Communist countries will receive an influx of Western comics to spur their industry into further action.

The Scandinavian countries have had their share of successes in the comics field. 1902 saw the first Swedish comic strip, *Mannen Som Gor Vad Som Faller Honom In* (The Man Who Does Whatever Comes to His Mind) by Oskar Andersson (OA). Many comics read in Scandinavia in the twentieth century, however, were of American or European origins; the first American series was imported as far back as 1906.

In 1920 Sweden achieved worldwide success with *Adamson* (known as *Silent Sam* in the USA) by Oscar Jacobsson. Appearing in the humour weekly **Sondags-Nisse** (Sunday Troll), *Adamson* was a witty and bizarre pantomime strip which outlived its creator, who died in 1945, and went on to delight and amuse its Swedish readers until 1965, drawn by Viggo Ludvigsen. Also in 1965, the Swedish Academy for Comic Strips was established to

provide research and encouragement for the comic field.

The rest of Scandinavia also contributed to the comics tradition. In 1925 the famous Finnish comic strip *Pekka Puupaa* (Peter Blockhead) began its fifty-year-run in the co-operative magazine **Kuluttajain Lehti**. Drawn by cartoonist Ola Fogelberg, the strip propagated leftist ideas as well as exposing human weaknesses in general.

In 1949, Finnish artist Tove Jansson created the fantasy series *Mumin* (Moomin) with its roots firmly planted in European fairy tales. This lovable series was successful worldwide and has been adapted for radio, puppet and television films in Germany and elsewhere.

Two other popular Scandinavian strips of recent years are *Petzi, Pelle, Pingo* by V. Hansen and *Rickard och hans Katt* (Richard and His Cat). The former strip is again reminiscent of fairy tales while the latter tells the adventures of a young boy and his cat in the big city.

The Latin American scene

Comics got off to an early start in the South and Central American countries with **O Tico Tico Comic** in Brazil in 1905 and American *Mutt and Jeff* reprints reaching Argentina as early as 1910.

Argentina had its first original newspaper strip, *El Negro Raul* by Arturo Lanteri, published in 1916 in the Buenos Aires magazine **El Hogar**. *El Negro Raul* was a pioneering strip by any standards, which related the frustrations and the bitter moral lessons to be learned by a black man trying to survive in a racist and hostile city.

Lanteri's work was destined to be brilliantly innovative and he dominated the Argentinian comic strip

whom Argentinian males could easily relate, and his exploits were depicted in Argentina's first talking film, directed by Lanteri in 1931.

An even longer-running strip of the period was Lino Palacio's *Don Fulgencio o el Hombre que no Tuvo Infancia* (Mr Fulgencio, or the Man Who Had No Childhood). *Don Fulgencio* began in 1935 and became the most popular strip in the country; he has since been adapted to screen and radio. Making his début in **La Opinion**, *Don Fulgencio* moved to **La Prensa** in 1939 and later to **La Razon** where he continued his over forty-year run. A dreamer at heart, *Don Fulgencio* spent his time recreating the childhood he never had. His trappings of respectability, all hard-earned, are tossed aside at every opportunity in an effort

by Enrique Rapela, an artist who was later to become famous for his portrayal of the hard life of the pampas and the gauchos' exploits.

One of Argentina's first quality adventure strips saw the light of day in 1936 in the comic magazine **Patoruzu**. *Hernan el Corsario* (Hernan the Privateer) was created by José-Luis Salinas and was a portent of the great things to come from one of Argentina's most talented graphic stylists.

Salinas was the first choice of King Features when they decided to publish their *Cisco Kid* strip, based on O. Henry's Western story and the popular series of *Cisco Kid* movies in the 1930s. Salinas obliged with some of the best Western art to be seen in comics. His panels were full

Argentina's mischievous and childish Don Fulgencio *by Lino Palacio soon became the country's most popular strip*

Arturo Del Castillo transformed the Randall *Western strip into an allegorical epic. First appearing in 1957 in Argentina,* Randall *was scripted by Hector Oesterheld*

scene throughout its early years. *El Negro Raul* finished in the early 1920s when Lanteri went on to create his most popular strip, *Don Pancho Talero*, which ran in **El Hogar** from 1922 to 1944. While similar in idea to *Bringing up Father*, *Don Pancho Talero*'s roots were firmly planted in Argentinian middle-class life. *Talero*, dominated by his overbearing wife, was a character to

to recapture the youth that he had sacrificed to become successful.

The Argentinians have long been avid fans of tales of the North American West and in 1931 Jose Vidal Davila created their first Western strip, *Douglas Watson*, the adventures of a Canadian Mountie. This was soon followed by *El Rey de las Praderas* (The King of the Prairies)

of motion and his vistas of the Western landscapes realistically breathtaking. The strip ran in American newspapers from 1951 to 1968.

During the 1940s, South American comic production diminished as a result of American imports. The next decade, however, saw the creation of another excellent Argentinian Western strip in *Sgt Kirk*.

Created by the prolific writer and editor Hector Oesterheld, this off-beat strip was drawn by Italian artist Hugo Pratt who was living in Argentina at the time. Other Oesterheld Westerns of the decade included *Ticonderoga*, also drawn by Pratt, and *Verduga Ranch*, drawn by Pavone.

Possibly the best classic Western of them all was the superlative *Randall* (1957) with art by Chilean-born Arturo Del Castillo, a draftsman whose talent was most certainly on a par with that of Salinas. Set in the post-Civil War West, *Randall* transcended the other strips in the genre due to Del Castillo's incisive compositions and skilful penwork. Del Castillo went on to delineate *Garret* in 1962, *Larrigan* and *Ringo* in 1964, as well as *Dan Dakota* and *El Cobra* in the 1970s.

In 1964 Argentina gave birth to *Mafalda*, a humorous and insightful strip about an argumentative little girl and her views on the world situation. A Latin version of *Peanuts*, *Mafalda* was tremendously successful and spawned a vast amount of merchandising which included animated cartoons for television. Her views have been translated into six languages and were published widely throughout Europe and Latin America.

The South American countries have always had a great enthusiasm for comics and have produced a number of fine artists and writers, many of whom have worked for American and European publishers such as Marvel and IPC. The trend for adult comics in Latin countries is now well established, with strips such as Brazil's *Noite Negra* by Nico Rosso and Argentina's *El Viage mas Largo* by Saccomano and Zanotto, *Alvar Mayor* by Carlos Trillo and Alberto Breccia, and *Merdichesky* by Trillo and Horacio Altuna, encompassing sex, violence and black magic in a Latin tradition.

A scene from Guillermo Saccomano and Juan Zanotto's El Viaje más Largo (The Longest Trip) *shows an astronaut, caught in a time warp, meeting Death in her many forms*

The Filipino factor

But perhaps one of the most surprising contributors to the comics field, though dwarfed in size by the Latin American countries, is the Philippines. With a population of fifty-four million people, the Philippines can lay claim to possessing some of the most avid comic readers in the world. This enthusiasm for the genre is reflected in the size and the quality of their own indigenous output of comics.

With the introduction in 1929 of *Kenkoy*, the most popular Philippine cartoon character ever, the Philippine comics were launched in style. Appearing in **Liwayway** publications, *Kenkoy* was the brainchild of Tony Velasquez, an artist, writer and editor who is considered the father of the Philippine comics industry. *Kenkoy* himself was a typical Filipino teenager whose efforts to cope with growing up, marriage and children were humorously portrayed over many years as the strip evolved into a family feature of warmth and wit. There was a *Kenkoy* movie as well as numerous merchandising offshoots from this phenomenally successful series.

Throughout the Thirties and Forties the comics of the Philippines were dominated by jungle strips including *Kulafu*, the Filipino *Tarzan* who made his début in **Bannawag** in 1934, drawn by Francisco Reyes Senior. In the same year *Marabini*, the jungle girl, appeared in **Liwayway**. These were the forerunners of a host of jungle strips including *Hagibis*, *Dumagit*, *Diwani* and *Og*, to name but a few.

Filipino artists later drew jungle strips in a variety of American comics and newspapers. One of the most noteworthy was Nestor Redondo's *Rima* strip for DC comics.

In the late 1940s Ramon Roces established Ace Publications which dominated the Philippine comics scene for the next several decades. With the publication of **Pilipino Komiks** in 1947, Ace Publications went on to produce **Hiwaga, Tagalog Klasiks, Educational Klasiks** and **Kenkoy Komiks**, among others. With Tony Velasquez, Francisco Reyes, Carlos Francisco, Francisco V. Coching and Alfredo Alcala in the Ace stable of artists and writers, the comics of the country went from strength to strength.

El Indio, *written and illustrated by F.V. Coching, first appeared in* **Pilipino Komiks** *in 1953. Charged with gripping and emotional sequences, the stories ran for over 30 chapters*

Alfredo Alcala went on to produce some of the finest comic work to come out of the Philippines. His astonishing **Voltar** epic, beginning in 1963, constituted a true masterpiece of detailed art and imagination. Based on a combination of myths, legends and actual history, the **Voltar** graphic novel presented brooding landscapes and exciting adventures which drew the reader into an unforgettable world of mythological splendour.

The catalogue of Ace writers and artists over the years reads like an encyclopedia of expertise. To touch but the tip of the iceberg, some of the classic strips produced by the country's artists include *Satur*, *Lapu-Lapu*, *Kalabog en Bosyo*, *El Indio*, *Maldita* and *Buntot-Page*. The Philippines have proved to be fertile ground for a wealth of talent and their comics are acclaimed the world over.

There is no doubt that comic production around the world has evolved dramatically over the past few decades. A new sophistication aimed at the teenage and adult markets has opened the field to subjects and techniques of expression not previously seen in the genre. Each country has had something worthwhile to contribute, notably for quality and inventiveness rather than simple imitation of US comics. The comics have proved themselves to be a more than worthy medium for breaking down the barriers between nations. They speak a language that everyone understands and they will continue to educate and entertain the world population with ever-increasing acceptance.

The extraordinary Voltar *series was entirely the work of one man: Alfredo P. Alcala created* Voltar *for the first issue of* **Alcala Fight Komik** *in 1963 and the eventual graphic-novel is deemed a masterpiece of the genre*

Select Bibliography

Benton, Mike
The Comic Book in America
Taylor Publishing Company, USA 1989

Bell, John
Canuck Comics
Matrix Books, Canada 1986

Chinese Comics Exhibition Catalogue
China Exhibition Agency

English Caricature 1620 to the Present
The Victoria and Albert Museum, UK 1984

Feiffer, Jules
The Great Comic Book Heroes
Dial Press/Allen Lane, USA 1965;
Penguin Press, UK 1967

Gerber, Ernst and Mary
The Photo-Journal Guide to Comicbooks
Gerber Publishing Company Inc, USA 1989

Gifford, Denis
The American Comic Book Catalogue
Mansell Publishing Ltd, UK 1990

Goulart, Ron
The Encyclopedia of American Comics
Facts on File/Promised Land, USA 1990:
The Great Comic Book Artists Volume 2
St Martin's Press, USA 1989:
Great History of Comic Books
Contempory Books Inc, USA 1986

Gravett, Paul and Stanbury, Peter (eds)
Escape Magazine (various issues)
Titan Books Ltd, UK

Horn, Maurice,
Comics of the American West
Staegan Publishing Co, USA, 1977:
Sex in the Comics (ed)
Chelsea House Publishers, USA 1985:
The World Encyclopedia of Comics (ed)
Chelsea House Publishers, USA 1976

Hurlmann, Bettina
Three Centuries of Children's Books in Europe
Oxford University Press, England 1967

Jacobs, Will, and Jones, Gerard
The Comic Book Heroes
Crown Publishers Inc, USA 1985

Kane, Bob, with Andrave, Tom
Batman and Me
Eclipse Books, USA 1989

Nemo (magazine), Issues 1 − 30
Fantagraphics Books Inc, USA
June 1983 − April 1989

Overstreet, Robert M.
Comic Book Price Guide
The House of Collectibles, USA 1991

Perry, George, and Aldridge, Alan
The Penguin Book of Comics
Penguin Books, UK 1967/1971

Print Magazine XLII:VI
Robert Cadel, USA 1988

Reitberger, Reinhold, and Fuchs, Wolfgang
Comics: Anatomy of a Mass Medium
Studio Vista Publishers, UK 1972

Schodt, Frederick L.
Manga! Manga! The World of Japanese Comics
Kodansha International Ltd, Japan, 1983

Sheridan, Martin
Classic Comics and their Creators
Post-era Books, USA 1942/1973

Wooley, Charles
Wooley's History of the Comic Book 1899 − 1936
Charles Wooley, USA 1986

Acknowledgements

All the illustrations in this book are reproduced as historical illustrations to the text. Grateful acknowledgement is made to the publishers and artists without whose contribution this book would not have been possible. The authors are especially indebted to the following for permission to reproduce copyright material:

All material originally published by D.C. Thomson & Co. Ltd. is reprinted by permission of D.C. Thomson & Co. Ltd

Super Lopez
© Ediciones B, S.A./Jan

Zipi y Zape
© Ediciones B, S.A./Encobar

Rubert Bear illustrations
© Express Newspapers plc.

Cerebus illustration
© Dave Sim and Frank Thorne

Tintin illustrations
© Herge/Casterman

Viz Illustration reproduced with permission from House of Viz

Gerald G. Swan comics
(Alan Clark)

Chico Bento/A Turma do Arrepio
© Editora Globo S/A − Brasil
all rights reserved

All material originally published by Fleetway Publications is reprinted by permission of Fleetway Publications

All Marvel characters and the distinctive likeness thereof are trademarks of the Marvel Entertainment Group, Inc. and are used with permission
© 1991 Marvel Entertainement Group, Inc. All rights reserved.

Conan the Barbarian appears by kind permission of Lieberman, Rudolph and Nowak.

All DC Comics characters, related logos and indicia are trademarked and copyrighted by DC Comics Inc. Illustrations 1938, 1941, 1942, 1944, 1946, 1947, 1949, 1950, 1952, 1954, 1956, 1957, 1958, 1959, 1960 © DC Comics Inc. Cover illustration Batman No 10 © 1942 DC Comics Inc. All rights reserved.

Although every effort has been made to trace the owners of copyright material, in a few cases this has not proved possible and the publishers would be grateful to receive notice of any copyright material that may have been overlooked.

Index